# LOW-LEVEL SYSTEMS PROGRAMMING WITH MACHINE AND ASSEMBLY LANGUAGE

Building High-Performance Software with Direct Hardware Interaction

# NATHAN WESTWOOD

# TABLE OF CONTENTS

# ABOUT THE AUTHOR!

## Dr. Nathan Westwood

**Biography:**

Dr. Nathan Westwood is a pioneering technologist known for his exceptional contributions to the fields of software development, cloud computing, and artificial intelligence. With a passion for innovation and a relentless drive to solve complex problems, Nathan has become a prominent figure in the tech industry, shaping the future of digital technology.

Born and raised in Silicon Valley, Nathan's interest in technology started at a young age. His fascination with computers and coding led him to pursue a degree in Computer Science from Stanford University, where he excelled academically and honed his skills in programming and software engineering. During his time at Stanford, Nathan was involved in several cutting-edge projects that sparked his interest in AI and cloud technologies.

After graduating, Nathan joined a leading tech firm where he played a key role in developing cloud-based solutions that revolutionized data storage and analytics. His work in the early stages of cloud computing set the foundation for modern infrastructure-as-a-service (IaaS) platforms, earning him recognition as one of the industry's emerging stars. As a lead engineer, Nathan was instrumental in launching products that have since become industry standards.

Nathan's entrepreneurial spirit led him to co-found his own tech startup focused on AI-driven automation tools for businesses. Under his leadership, the company rapidly gained traction, attracting both investors and clients who were eager to leverage his innovative AI solutions to streamline operations and improve efficiency. Nathan's commitment to pushing the boundaries of what's possible in tech quickly earned him a reputation as a visionary leader.

Known for his expertise in machine learning, Nathan has also worked with several large tech companies, advising on the integration of AI and data science into their operations. His work has spanned various sectors, including healthcare, finance, and manufacturing, where he has helped organizations harness the power of data and automation to achieve exponential growth.

Beyond his technical achievements, Nathan is a sought-after speaker at global tech conferences, where he shares his insights on the future of cloud computing, artificial intelligence, and the ethical challenges posed by emerging technologies. His thought leadership and commitment to ethical innovation have made him a respected voice in the tech community.

In addition to his professional accomplishments, Nathan is deeply passionate about mentoring the next generation of tech leaders. He regularly contributes to educational programs and initiatives designed to inspire young minds and equip them with the skills necessary to thrive in the ever-evolving tech landscape.

Nathan Westwood continues to be a trailblazer in the tech industry, shaping the future of technology with his innovative ideas, entrepreneurial spirit, and commitment to making a positive impact on the world.

# Chapter 1: Introduction to Low-Level Systems Programming

## 1.1 WHAT IS LOW-LEVEL SYSTEMS PROGRAMMING?

Low-level systems programming is a branch of programming that involves writing software that interacts directly with the hardware of a computer system. Unlike higher-level programming, where abstractions like objects, classes, and libraries hide the underlying hardware, low-level programming is focused on managing and utilizing the resources of the machine as efficiently as possible.

At its core, low-level programming involves working close to the machine, directly manipulating memory, processor registers, and hardware components. It provides the foundation for operating systems, embedded systems, device drivers, and other critical software that needs to maximize performance and efficiency.

In low-level programming, the programmer has full control over the system's resources. For example, when you write code in high-level languages like Python or Java, the underlying system is abstracted away, and you rely on the operating system to manage memory and I/O operations. In contrast, low-level programming allows you to take direct control of these operations, offering unmatched speed and efficiency but at the cost of complexity and more detailed management of hardware resources.

## 1.2 THE RELATIONSHIP BETWEEN HARDWARE AND SOFTWARE IN LOW-LEVEL PROGRAMMING

In low-level programming, understanding the relationship between hardware and software is essential. The hardware provides the raw computing power, while the software provides the instructions to tell the hardware what to do. The bridge between these two is what makes low-level systems programming so powerful.

At the most fundamental level, hardware consists of components like the **CPU**, **memory**, and **I/O devices** (e.g., disk drives, keyboards, and screens). The CPU executes instructions, and memory stores data that the CPU operates on. The **bus** connects all these components, allowing them to communicate.

Software, on the other hand, consists of programs (like operating systems, applications, or device drivers) that provide instructions to the hardware. Low-level programming is about writing software that controls the hardware components directly, bypassing the abstractions provided by higher-level languages or operating systems.

For example, when writing code that interacts with memory, low-level programmers must manage memory addresses, ensure proper allocation, and optimize the use of memory without the automatic garbage collection that high-level languages provide. Similarly, low-level code often involves writing device drivers to manage and communicate with peripheral devices, like printers, network cards, and disk drives.

## 1.3 INTRODUCTION TO MACHINE LANGUAGE AND ASSEMBLY LANGUAGE

Machine language is the most basic programming language that a computer understands. It is composed entirely of binary digits (0s and 1s), representing the instructions that tell the CPU what to do. Each instruction in machine language is designed to perform a specific task, such as moving data from one memory location to another or performing arithmetic calculations.

However, machine language is not human-readable. To make things easier for programmers, assembly language was developed. Assembly language is a symbolic representation of machine code. It uses human-readable mnemonics like MOV, ADD, and JMP to represent machine instructions.

The key difference between machine language and assembly language is that assembly language is easier for humans to write and read, while machine language is directly executed by the CPU. However, the CPU still requires machine code to operate, so assembly language needs to be converted into machine code by an assembler before execution.

**Why is understanding machine and assembly languages crucial for high-performance systems?**

1. **Control over Hardware**: Understanding these languages allows developers to control the hardware directly, making it possible to optimize performance in ways that higher-level languages cannot.
2. **Memory Management**: Low-level programming gives developers the ability to manage memory manually, which is important in systems where memory is limited (e.g., embedded systems).

3. **Speed and Efficiency**: Since low-level languages allow direct access to hardware, programs written in these languages can run faster and consume less memory than those written in high-level languages.

---

## 1.4 THE ROLE OF LOW-LEVEL PROGRAMMING IN MODERN COMPUTING SYSTEMS

Low-level programming plays a critical role in many modern computing systems, including:

1. **Operating Systems (OS)**: The operating system is the interface between hardware and user applications. It manages hardware resources and provides services such as file systems, memory management, and process scheduling. Operating systems are often written in low-level languages, especially for embedded systems or when high performance is critical. For instance, the kernel (the heart of the operating system) is written in C, which is considered a low-level language due to its proximity to assembly.
2. **Embedded Systems**: Embedded systems are specialized computing systems designed to perform specific tasks, like controlling household appliances or automotive systems. These systems often operate with limited resources (memory, processing power) and require low-level programming to ensure efficiency and reliability.
3. **Robotics**: Low-level programming is used extensively in robotics. From controlling motors and sensors to managing power consumption, robots require precise control of hardware components. Many robotic systems use assembly or C for real-time control and optimization of hardware operations.

4. **Device Drivers**: A device driver is a piece of software that allows the operating system to communicate with hardware devices. Drivers must interact directly with the hardware, and thus, low-level programming is required to ensure correct, efficient operation.
5. **Networking**: Low-level programming is used to implement networking protocols and drivers. Systems that require high-speed data transfer or low-latency communication often use low-level code to maximize efficiency.
6. **Game Engines**: In gaming, real-time performance is critical. Low-level programming is used to write graphics rendering code, physics simulations, and even the game engine itself. Games often need to run at a high frame rate, and low-level code ensures this by accessing the hardware directly.

## 1.5 Hands-On Example: Writing Your First "Hello, World!" in Assembly

Now that we've covered the theory, let's dive into our first hands-on example: writing a simple "Hello, World!" program in assembly.

To begin with, you'll need an assembler to translate your assembly code into machine code. For this example, we'll use **NASM (Netwide Assembler),** a popular assembler for x86 architecture.

1. **Step 1: Install NASM**
   o   On Linux, you can install NASM via the terminal using the command:

```arduino
sudo apt-get install nasm
```

2. **Step 2: Writing the Code**
   - Open a text editor and write the following assembly code:

   ```assembly
   ; HelloWorld.asm
   section .data
   hello db 'Hello, World!', 0

   section .text
   global _start

   _start:
       ; write our string to stdout
       mov eax, 4          ; system call
   number for sys_write
       mov ebx, 1          ; file descriptor
   1 is stdout
       mov ecx, hello      ; pointer to our
   string
       mov edx, 13         ; length of the
   string
       int 0x80            ; interrupt to
   make the system call

       ; exit the program
       mov eax, 1          ; system call
   number for sys_exit
       xor ebx, ebx        ; exit code 0
       int 0x80            ; interrupt to
   make the system call
   ```

3. **Step 3: Assemble and Link the Code**
   - Save the file as `HelloWorld.asm`. Now, open your terminal and assemble the code:

   ```bash
   nasm -f elf32 HelloWorld.asm
   ```

   - Link the object file to create an executable:

```bash
ld -m elf_i386 -s -o HelloWorld
HelloWorld.o
```

4. **Step 4: Run the Program**
   o Finally, run the program:

```bash
./HelloWorld
```

   o You should see the output:

```
Hello, World!
```

Congratulations! You've just written your first assembly program. This example may seem simple, but it introduces several key concepts in low-level programming, such as system calls, memory management, and interacting with the operating system.

---

## 1.6 SUMMARY

Low-level systems programming is a powerful and indispensable skill for developers working on performance-critical systems. By writing code that directly interacts with hardware, programmers can achieve superior performance and control, making it essential for developing operating systems, embedded systems, and real-time applications.

In this chapter, we've introduced the fundamental concepts of low-level programming, including the relationship between hardware and software, machine and assembly languages, and the crucial role that low-level code plays in modern computing systems. We also walked through a hands-on example where you wrote your first "Hello, World!" program in assembly.

This chapter has set the foundation for the more advanced topics and hands-on projects that will follow in this book, and you should now have a clearer understanding of what low-level programming is, why it matters, and how to get started.

Stay tuned for the next chapter, where we'll explore the assembly language instruction set and build on the concepts we've learned today!

# Chapter 2: The Basics of Machine Language

## 2.1 Understanding Machine Code: Binary and Hexadecimal Representation

When we talk about machine language, we are diving into the raw instructions that a computer's CPU understands. At its core, machine language consists entirely of binary digits, or "bits," represented by the numbers 0 and 1. These bits are the building blocks of all information in computing, including the instructions that tell the CPU what to do.

**Why Binary?** The choice of binary is rooted in the fact that computers use electrical circuits to represent data. Each bit can be either in an "off" state (0) or an "on" state (1), making it ideal for digital electronics. This "on/off" concept corresponds directly to the voltage states within the circuits of the CPU.

**Binary Representation** A single bit can only hold one of two possible values: 0 or 1. A group of 8 bits is known as a **byte**, which is the smallest addressable unit of memory in most systems. For example:

- A byte: `11001010`

However, humans typically don't deal with raw binary code directly because it's long, cumbersome, and prone to errors. Instead, we often use **hexadecimal** (base-16) notation as a shorthand. Each hexadecimal digit represents exactly 4 bits. Here's a quick comparison:

- Binary: 11001010
- Hexadecimal: CA

In hexadecimal, the digits 0–9 represent values from 0 to 9, while A–F represent values from 10 to 15. This makes reading binary much easier because you need fewer digits.

For instance, to represent the binary string 111100001110000011111000, it's much easier to write this in hexadecimal as F0E0F0. This shorthand helps programmers understand and debug machine code more efficiently.

---

## 2.2 THE CPU'S ROLE IN EXECUTING MACHINE CODE

The **CPU** (Central Processing Unit) is the brain of any computer. It's the hardware component responsible for interpreting and executing machine code instructions. The CPU doesn't inherently "understand" human-readable code like Python or JavaScript. Instead, it only understands machine code—the raw binary or hexadecimal instructions that control its operations.

### How Does the CPU Execute Machine Code?

When machine code is executed, it follows a process called the **fetch-decode-execute cycle**, which consists of three main stages:

1. **Fetch:** The CPU retrieves an instruction from memory (RAM). It looks at the instruction stored at the memory address

pointed to by the **program counter** (PC). The program counter keeps track of where the CPU is in its instruction sequence.

2. **Decode**: The CPU decodes the instruction to determine what action needs to be taken. The instruction could be anything from adding two numbers to reading from memory. The CPU's **decoder unit** takes care of translating the instruction into a series of actions the CPU can execute.

3. **Execute**: The CPU performs the operation specified by the instruction. This might involve arithmetic operations (like addition or subtraction), data movement (moving data from one place in memory to another), or control operations (like jumping to another part of the program).

The CPU uses a set of registers—small, fast storage locations inside the CPU—to hold data temporarily. For example, when you execute an addition instruction, the operands (the numbers being added) are first loaded into these registers. The result is stored back in one of these registers or in memory.

The CPU is designed to perform these steps quickly and repeatedly, making it seem like it's running complex programs instantly. However, everything that happens inside the computer, from loading data from storage to rendering images on your screen, is just a sequence of machine code instructions being executed by the CPU.

## 2.3 How Low-Level Code Interacts Directly with the Hardware

Low-level programming is all about interacting directly with the hardware of the system. While high-level programming languages like Python or Java allow developers to focus on logic and algorithms without worrying about the underlying hardware, low-level programming requires detailed management of system resources.

**Memory Management**

When you write low-level code, you have to think about how to allocate, access, and free up memory manually. In high-level languages, this process is automated through garbage collection. But in low-level programming, it's your responsibility to track memory addresses and ensure the system doesn't run out of memory or accidentally overwrite data.

For instance, if you need to store a number in memory, you must specify the memory address where this value should go. This is typically done using pointers—variables that store the memory address of another variable.

**Input/Output (I/O) Operations**

Low-level code also allows you to interact directly with input/output devices, like the keyboard, screen, or disk drive. High-level programming provides abstractions for these tasks, such as libraries for file handling or screen drawing. In low-level systems programming, you might write the code that communicates directly with the hardware controllers that manage these devices.

**Instruction Set Architecture (ISA)**

The way low-level code interacts with the hardware depends heavily on the **Instruction Set Architecture** (ISA) of the CPU. The ISA defines the set of instructions that the CPU understands and can execute. Different CPUs have different ISAs. For example, Intel and AMD CPUs typically use the **x86** or **x86-64** ISA, while ARM processors (common in mobile devices) use a completely different set of instructions.

An understanding of the ISA is crucial when writing low-level code because the machine instructions that control the hardware will be different depending on the CPU's architecture.

---

## 2.4 HANDS-ON EXAMPLE: WRITING BASIC MACHINE CODE INSTRUCTIONS AND RUNNING THEM IN A SIMULATOR

Now that we understand the theory, it's time for a hands-on example. We'll write a simple program that performs an addition of two numbers using machine code. To keep things accessible, we'll work with an **x86** architecture, which is widely used in PCs.

We will use an **emulator** to simulate the execution of the program, which allows us to see how machine code works without needing to interact with actual hardware.

### Step 1: Writing the Machine Code

Let's say we want to add the numbers 5 and 3. We can write the following simple machine instructions:

1. **Load the first number (5) into a register.**
2. **Load the second number (3) into a second register.**
3. **Add the contents of the two registers.**
4. **Store the result back into memory.**

In binary, the machine code instructions might look like this:

- MOV AL, 5 (Move the value 5 into register AL)
- MOV BL, 3 (Move the value 3 into register BL)

- `ADD AL, BL` (Add the contents of `AL` and `BL`, storing the result in `AL`)

These instructions are already in assembly language, which is human-readable but still represents machine instructions. Now, we need to convert these instructions into machine code.

## Step 2: Converting Assembly to Machine Code

The assembler converts the assembly code into machine code. Here's a breakdown of how the instructions might convert:

- `MOV AL, 5`: This instruction could translate to the binary code `10111000 00000101` (in hexadecimal, `B0 05`).
- `MOV BL, 3`: This might translate to `10111001 00000011` (in hexadecimal, `B3 03`).
- `ADD AL, BL`: This could translate to `00000001 11000111` (in hexadecimal, `01 C3`).

When we put it all together, our program might look like this in machine code:

```nginx
B0 05 B3 03 01 C3
```

## Step 3: Running the Code in a Simulator

To run this machine code, we can use an emulator like **EMU8086** or **DOSBox**, which simulates the x86 architecture on a modern machine.

1. **Open the emulator** and create a new file.
2. **Enter the machine code** directly (or use an assembler to generate it and load it into the emulator).
3. **Run the program**: The emulator will simulate the CPU executing the machine instructions step by step.

You should see that the program adds 5 and 3, and the result 8 is stored in the AL register (which can be viewed in the emulator's debugger).

---

## 2.5 SUMMARY

In this chapter, we explored the fundamentals of machine language, the binary and hexadecimal representations used to encode machine code instructions, and how the CPU executes these instructions to perform tasks. We also covered how low-level code interacts with the hardware directly, allowing for fine-grained control over the system's resources, memory, and I/O devices.

The hands-on example provided an introduction to writing machine code instructions in assembly, translating them to machine code, and running them in an emulator to observe how they execute on a simulated CPU. This experience is crucial for understanding how computers execute instructions at the most fundamental level.

As we move forward, we'll continue building on these concepts to explore more advanced machine code operations, as well as how to optimize and debug low-level code in real-world applications.

# Chapter 3: Introduction to Assembly Language

## 3.1 THE DIFFERENCE BETWEEN ASSEMBLY AND MACHINE LANGUAGE

Before diving into the specifics of assembly language, it's crucial to understand the difference between **assembly language** and **machine language,** as these two terms are often confused but are fundamentally distinct.

1. **Machine Language**: This is the lowest-level programming language, consisting entirely of binary instructions (0s and 1s) that the CPU directly executes. Machine language is specific to the CPU architecture and is incredibly difficult for humans to read or write manually. It's often represented in binary or hexadecimal format for ease of understanding, but each instruction directly corresponds to an operation that the CPU performs.
2. **Assembly Language**: Assembly language is a step above machine language in terms of readability. It uses **mnemonics**, which are short and meaningful names for machine instructions. For example:
   - MOV for move (transfer data)
   - ADD for add (perform addition)
   - JMP for jump (control flow)

   These mnemonics represent specific machine code instructions, but they make it easier for humans to write and understand programs. Assembly language is also specific to the CPU architecture, but it is much more readable than machine code. However, it still needs to be converted into machine code by an **assembler** before execution.

**Key Takeaway**: While machine language consists entirely of binary numbers, assembly language is a human-readable alternative where instructions are represented by mnemonic codes. Assembly serves as a convenient way to write machine code more efficiently, making it easier to manage the details of the system.

---

## 3.2 ASSEMBLY LANGUAGE SYNTAX AND STRUCTURE

Now that we've established the difference between assembly and machine language, it's time to explore the structure of assembly language itself. Understanding this structure will help you start writing programs that interact directly with the hardware.

**Basic Structure of an Assembly Program**
An assembly program is made up of several distinct sections that tell the CPU what to do. These sections include:

1.  **Data Section**:
    This section is used to declare variables, constants, and memory locations that will hold data. The data section is where you store the information that the program will manipulate. For example, if you're working with integers or strings, you would define them here.

    Example:

    ```assembly
    assembly

    section .data
    ```

```
num1 db 5            ; Declare a byte with the
value 5
num2 db 10           ; Declare a byte with the
value 10
```

2. **Text Section**:
   The text section contains the instructions that the CPU will execute. This is where the actual program logic goes. The text section is the heart of your program.

   Example:

   assembly

```
section .text
global _start        ; Declare the entry point
for the program

_start:
     ; Program instructions go here
```

3. **Registers**:
   Assembly language interacts heavily with **registers**, which are small, fast storage locations in the CPU. Registers temporarily store data that the CPU operates on. For example, you might load a number into a register, perform some arithmetic operation on it, and then store the result back in memory.

   The most commonly used registers are:

   o **AX, BX, CX, DX**: General-purpose registers
   o **SI (Source Index), DI (Destination Index)**: Used for string operations
   o **SP (Stack Pointer)**: Points to the top of the stack
   o **BP (Base Pointer)**: Used for referencing function parameters

4. **Instructions**:
   Assembly language instructions are typically one word long
   and correspond to specific machine operations. Some
   common instructions are:
   - MOV: Move data from one place to another
   - ADD: Add two values
   - SUB: Subtract one value from another
   - JMP: Jump to another instruction (used for control
     flow)
   - CMP: Compare two values

**Example: A Basic Program**

```assembly
section .data
num1 db 10          ; Declare a byte with value 10
num2 db 20          ; Declare a byte with value 20

section .text
global _start

_start:
    mov al, [num1]      ; Load value from num1 into
register AL
    add al, [num2]      ; Add value from num2 to AL
    ; AL now holds 30 (10 + 20)

    ; End the program
    mov eax, 1          ; System call number for exit
    int 0x80            ; Interrupt to exit the
program
```

In this program:

- The **data section** defines two variables, num1 and num2.
- The **text section** contains instructions that move values into
  registers, add them, and then exit the program.

## 3.3 REGISTERS, MEMORY ADDRESSING, AND STACK OPERATIONS

To fully understand assembly language, it's crucial to know how registers, memory addressing, and the stack work. These elements are the building blocks that allow programs to interact with memory and perform various tasks.

1. **Registers and Their Role**
   Registers are tiny but extremely fast storage locations inside the CPU. When you run an assembly program, the CPU uses registers to hold data while performing calculations or moving data around. Registers can hold a variety of data types, such as integers, pointers, and addresses.

   For example:

   - `MOV AX, 5` stores the value 5 in the `AX` register.
   - `MOV BX, AX` copies the contents of `AX` into `BX`.

   **Common Registers in x86:**

   - **EAX**: Accumulator register, often used for arithmetic operations.
   - **EBX**: Base register, typically used for memory addressing.
   - **ECX**: Count register, used in loop operations.
   - **EDX**: Data register, often used in I/O operations.

2. **Memory Addressing**
   In low-level programming, understanding how to address memory is critical. Memory is typically represented by a long list of byte addresses, starting from address `0x00000000` (the beginning of memory) and extending upward.

   There are different ways to address memory in assembly:

- o **Direct Addressing**: Accessing memory directly using a fixed address. Example:

assembly

```
mov al, [0x1234]    ; Load the byte from
memory address 0x1234 into AL
```

- o **Indirect Addressing**: Accessing memory using a pointer or register that holds an address. Example:

assembly

```
mov al, [bx]           ; Load the byte at
the address stored in BX into AL
```

**Example of Moving Data Using Memory Addressing**:

assembly

```
section .data
num1 db 15              ; Declare a byte with value
15

section .text
global _start

_start:
    mov al, [num1]     ; Load value of num1 into
AL
    add al, 10          ; Add 10 to AL
    ; AL now contains 25

    ; Exit the program
    mov eax, 1
    int 0x80
```

3. **The Stack**
   The stack is a special region of memory used for storing temporary data, like function parameters and local variables. It operates in a **Last-In-First-Out (LIFO)** manner,

meaning the last item pushed onto the stack is the first one to be popped off.

**Stack Operations:**

- **PUSH**: Adds a value to the stack.
- **POP**: Removes the top value from the stack.

The **stack pointer** (SP) keeps track of the current position of the stack. When data is pushed onto the stack, the stack pointer is decremented, and when data is popped, the stack pointer is incremented.

**Example of Stack Operations:**

```assembly
section .text
global _start

_start:
    push 5          ; Push 5 onto the stack
    push 10         ; Push 10 onto the stack
    pop ax          ; Pop the top value (10)
into register AX
    pop bx          ; Pop the next value (5)
into register BX

    ; AX = 10, BX = 5

    ; Exit the program
    mov eax, 1
    int 0x80
```

## 3.4 HANDS-ON EXAMPLE: WRITING SIMPLE ASSEMBLY PROGRAMS THAT MANIPULATE DATA IN REGISTERS

Now that we've discussed the core concepts of assembly language, let's dive into writing a simple assembly program that manipulates data in registers. In this example, we will:

1. Move values into registers.
2. Perform arithmetic operations.
3. Store the result in memory.
4. Exit the program.

<u>Example: Adding Two Numbers</u>

We'll write a simple program that adds two numbers and stores the result.

```
assembly

section .data
    num1 db 15          ; Declare a byte with value
15
    num2 db 10          ; Declare a byte with value
10
    result db 0         ; Declare a byte to store the
result

section .text
    global _start

_start:
    mov al, [num1]      ; Load value of num1 into AL
    add al, [num2]      ; Add value of num2 to AL (AL
= num1 + num2)
    mov [result], al    ; Store the result in the
'result' variable

    ; Exit the program
```

```
    mov eax, 1
    int 0x80                  ; Interrupt to exit the
program
```

In this example:

- We load the values of `num1` and `num2` into registers.
- We add the values in `num1` and `num2` and store the result in the `result` variable.
- We exit the program once the operation is complete.

You can run this program in an assembler and emulator to see how it executes and manipulates data in the registers.

---

# Conclusion

In this chapter, we've covered the basics of assembly language, from understanding its syntax and structure to exploring how registers, memory addressing, and stack operations work. Assembly language provides a closer connection to the hardware than high-level programming, allowing programmers to fine-tune the performance of their applications.

Through hands-on examples, we demonstrated how to write simple assembly programs, manipulate data in registers, and interact with memory. These are foundational skills for any programmer interested in low-level systems programming. In the next chapters, we'll continue building on these skills, diving deeper into advanced assembly programming techniques and optimizing code for real-world applications.

# Chapter 4: The Assembly Language Instruction Set

## 4.1 OVERVIEW OF COMMON ASSEMBLY INSTRUCTIONS

Assembly language instructions represent the actions that the CPU executes. These instructions are translated directly into machine code by an assembler, and each corresponds to an operation that the CPU can perform. In this chapter, we'll explore the most common types of assembly instructions used in low-level programming, their functions, and how they contribute to the overall operation of a program.

### 1. Data Movement Instructions

Data movement instructions are the foundation of most assembly programs. They allow data to be moved between registers, memory locations, and I/O ports.

- **MOV** (Move):
    - The MOV instruction is used to transfer data from one place to another. It is one of the most commonly used instructions in assembly programming.
    - Example:

```assembly
mov ax, 5      ; Move the value 5 into
register AX
```

Here, `AX` will hold the value 5 after the instruction is executed.

- **PUSH and POP**:
  - The `PUSH` instruction pushes a value onto the stack, and the `POP` instruction removes a value from the stack.
  - These instructions are useful for saving and restoring data, particularly when dealing with function calls and managing local variables.
  - Example:

```assembly
push ax        ; Push the value in AX onto the stack
pop bx         ; Pop the top value from the stack into BX
```

## 2. Arithmetic Instructions

Arithmetic instructions perform mathematical operations on data in registers or memory. These operations include addition, subtraction, multiplication, and division.

- **ADD**:
  - The `ADD` instruction adds the values in two registers or between a register and memory and stores the result in a destination register.
  - Example:

```assembly
add ax, bx     ; Add the value in BX to AX and store the result in AX
```

- **SUB**:
  - The `SUB` instruction subtracts the value in one register or memory location from another.

- Example:

```assembly
sub ax, bx      ; Subtract the value in BX
from AX and store the result in AX
```

- **MUL** and **IMUL**:
  - MUL performs unsigned multiplication, while IMUL performs signed multiplication.
  - Example:

```assembly
mul bx            ; Multiply AX by BX,
storing the result in DX:AX
```

- **DIV** and **IDIV**:
  - DIV divides the value in the AX register by the value in another register or memory location (for unsigned division), and IDIV is used for signed division.
  - Example:

```assembly
div bx            ; Divide AX by BX, storing
the result in AL and the remainder in AH
```

## 3. Control Flow Instructions

Control flow instructions manage the flow of execution within a program, allowing the program to make decisions, repeat tasks, or jump to other sections of code.

- **JMP** (Jump):
  - The JMP instruction causes the program to jump to another instruction, usually at a different location in memory.
  - Example:

```assembly
jmp label       ; Jump to the instruction
at 'label'
```

- **Conditional Jumps (e.g., JE, JNE, JG, JL):**
    - These instructions cause the program to jump only if certain conditions are met. For example, JE (Jump if Equal) will jump if two values are equal, while JNE (Jump if Not Equal) will jump if the values are not equal.
    - Example:

```assembly
je label        ; Jump to 'label' if zero
flag is set (i.e., values are equal)
jne label       ; Jump to 'label' if
values are not equal
```

- **CALL and RET:**
    - The CALL instruction is used to call a function (i.e., a subroutine), while RET is used to return from a function.
    - Example:

```assembly
call myFunction     ; Call a function
named 'myFunction'
ret                 ; Return from the
function
```

## 4.4 The Purpose of Data Movement, Arithmetic, and Control Flow Instructions

Data movement instructions handle the flow of data between registers, memory, and I/O, while arithmetic instructions perform operations on this data. Control flow instructions enable branching and jumping between different sections of a program based on conditions or function calls.

These instructions work together to form the core structure of any program. Without data movement, arithmetic, and control flow, a program wouldn't be able to manipulate data or make decisions.

## 4.2 THE USE OF FLAGS AND CONDITION CODES IN ASSEMBLY

In assembly language, flags and condition codes are special indicators set by the CPU that provide information about the outcome of various operations. These flags can influence how control flow instructions behave, such as whether or not the program should jump to a specific section of code.

### 1. What Are Flags?

Flags are binary indicators that hold a true or false value (1 or 0). The CPU uses them to represent the state of certain operations. For example, flags are set when certain conditions occur in arithmetic operations, such as when the result of a subtraction is zero or negative.

### 2. Common Flags in the x86 Architecture

- **Zero Flag (ZF):**
    - Set if the result of an operation is zero. For example, if AX is subtracted from BX and the result is 0, the Zero Flag will be set.
    - Example:

```assembly
cmp ax, bx      ; Compare AX with BX
je label        ; Jump if Zero Flag is set
(i.e., AX == BX)
```

- **Sign Flag (SF):**
    - o Set if the result of an operation is negative (i.e., the most significant bit is 1 in two's complement representation).
- **Carry Flag (CF):**
    - o Set if there is a carry-out from the most significant bit in addition, or if a borrow occurs in subtraction.
- **Overflow Flag (OF):**
    - o Set if an arithmetic overflow occurs, such as when the result of a signed operation exceeds the representable range.
- **Parity Flag (PF):**
    - o Set if the number of set bits (1s) in the result is even.

### 3. Using Flags in Conditional Jumps

Flags are essential when performing conditional jumps. These jumps occur based on the state of a flag, allowing the program to make decisions or repeat actions.

For instance, after performing a comparison using CMP (which is an alias for SUB), the CPU sets the appropriate flags, and conditional jump instructions can be used to control the program flow based on these flags.

**Example: Using the Zero Flag for a Conditional Jump**

```assembly
cmp ax, bx          ; Compare AX with BX
je equal_label      ; Jump if the Zero Flag is set (AX
== BX)
```

```
jne not_equal_label; Jump if the Zero Flag is not set
(AX != BX)
```

In this example:

- The CMP instruction performs the comparison and sets the Zero Flag if the values in AX and BX are equal.
- The program then jumps to equal_label if the values are equal or not_equal_label if they are not.

---

# 4.3 HANDS-ON EXAMPLE: BUILDING A SIMPLE CALCULATOR IN ASSEMBLY

Now that we've covered the basic instructions and flags, let's build a simple calculator that performs addition, subtraction, and multiplication in assembly. We will focus on user input and arithmetic operations, demonstrating how to manipulate data and control flow.

### Example: Simple Calculator in Assembly

This calculator will ask for two numbers, perform an arithmetic operation (addition, subtraction, or multiplication), and display the result. Since we are working in assembly, we will assume we have a basic understanding of how to handle input/output in a simplified console environment.

### Step 1: Declare Data and Get User Input

```
assembly

section .data
```

```
        prompt db 'Enter first number: ', 0   ; Prompt
message
        result db 'Result: ', 0                ; Result
message
        newline db 0x0A, 0                      ; Newline
for display

section .bss
        num1 resb 4      ; Reserve space for the first
number
        num2 resb 4      ; Reserve space for the second
number
        operation resb 1 ; Reserve space for the
operation (e.g., +, -, *)

section .text
        global _start

_start:
    ; Display prompt for the first number
        mov eax, 4                 ; System call for write
        mov ebx, 1                 ; File descriptor 1
(stdout)
        mov ecx, prompt            ; Address of the prompt
        mov edx, 18                ; Length of the prompt
string
        int 0x80                   ; Interrupt to execute
the system call

    ; Get user input for the first number
        mov eax, 3                 ; System call for read
        mov ebx, 0                 ; File descriptor 0
(stdin)
        mov ecx, num1              ; Address to store the
first number
        mov edx, 4                 ; Max length of input
        int 0x80                   ; Interrupt to execute
the system call

    ; Repeat similar steps to get second number and
operation...

    ; Perform addition
```

```
    ; Example for adding num1 and num2, storing in
result
    ; Assuming num1 and num2 are properly converted
to integers
    mov eax, [num1]              ; Load num1 into eax
    add eax, [num2]              ; Add num2 to eax
    mov [result], eax            ; Store result

    ; Display result (print it)
    mov eax, 4                   ; System call for write
    mov ebx, 1                   ; File descriptor 1
(stdout)
    mov ecx, result              ; Address of the result
    mov edx, 4                   ; Length of result
    int 0x80                     ; Interrupt to execute
the system call

    ; Exit the program
    mov eax, 1                   ; System call for exit
    xor ebx, ebx                 ; Exit with status 0
    int 0x80                     ; Interrupt to execute
the system call
```

## Step 2: Explaining the Operations

In this example, the program uses system calls to interact with the user:

- **write (system call 4)** to display text and the result.
- **read (system call 3)** to get user input.

We used simple arithmetic operations like ADD to perform the calculation. The result is then displayed back to the user.

# Conclusion

In this chapter, we've explored the core assembly language instructions that allow you to move data, perform arithmetic, and control program flow. We also discussed the importance of flags and condition codes in managing program execution.

Through a practical example, we demonstrated how to build a simple calculator that interacts with the user, manipulates data, and performs arithmetic operations.

Understanding these basic instructions is essential for any low-level programmer. In the next chapters, we will dive deeper into more complex concepts like memory management, optimization, and advanced system-level operations.

# Chapter 5: Data Representation and Memory Management

## 5.1 How Data Is Stored in Memory and Processed by the CPU

At the heart of any computing system is the concept of **data representation** and **memory management**. In low-level systems programming, understanding how data is stored in memory and processed by the CPU is essential for managing resources efficiently and building high-performance applications.

### 1. Binary Representation of Data

All data in a computer is ultimately represented as **binary numbers** (sequences of 0s and 1s), because the CPU operates on binary digits, or **bits**. These bits are grouped together into larger units, like **bytes** (8 bits), **words** (16 bits), **double words** (32 bits), and **quadwords** (64 bits). Each grouping has specific uses depending on the architecture and type of data being represented.

For example:

- **8-bit values**: Represent small integers or characters.
- **16-bit values**: Represent larger integers or short floating-point values.
- **32-bit values**: Represent even larger integers, floating-point numbers, or pointers in 32-bit systems.

- **64-bit values**: Used in modern architectures to represent larger integers, double-precision floating-point values, and larger address spaces.

## 2. How the CPU Interprets and Processes Data

The CPU's role is to execute instructions, and part of this process involves manipulating data in memory. The CPU can operate on data stored in registers, memory locations, or I/O devices. The data it processes is retrieved from memory through a process called **memory addressing**.

In a typical operation, the CPU:

1. Retrieves data from memory (or a register).
2. Executes the operation specified by an instruction (e.g., addition, subtraction, etc.).
3. Stores the result back into memory or a register.

For example, when adding two numbers, the CPU loads each number from memory into registers, performs the addition, and stores the result back in memory.

## 3. Little-Endian vs. Big-Endian Representation

Data representation also varies based on how multi-byte data (like a 32-bit integer) is stored in memory. The two primary formats for storing multi-byte data are:

- **Little-endian**: The least significant byte is stored first, at the lowest memory address. This is the format used by most x86 architectures.

  Example (32-bit integer 0x12345678):

o   Memory: `[0x78][0x56][0x34][0x12]`
- **Big-endian**: The most significant byte is stored first, at the lowest memory address. Some architectures, like older Motorola processors, use this format.

Example (32-bit integer `0x12345678`):

o   Memory: `[0x12][0x34][0x56][0x78]`

Understanding whether your system is little-endian or big-endian is important when handling binary data, especially when interacting with other systems or hardware devices that might use different conventions.

---

## 5.2 THE IMPORTANCE OF MEMORY ADDRESSING

Memory addressing is the way that the CPU references locations in memory to access or store data. The type of addressing scheme used depends on the architecture of the CPU, including whether it uses an **8-bit, 16-bit, 32-bit,** or **64-bit** address space. These different addressing schemes dictate how large the memory space is and how memory is accessed.

### 1. 8-bit, 16-bit, 32-bit, and 64-bit Architectures

In the world of assembly programming, understanding the difference between **8-bit, 16-bit, 32-bit,** and **64-bit architectures** is fundamental because it determines the size of memory that the CPU can address directly and the size of data it can process in one instruction.

- **8-bit Architecture:**
  In an 8-bit architecture, the CPU can address up to **256 memory locations** (2^8), typically using a **single byte** (8 bits) for data. This kind of architecture is limited in both data size and address space.
- **16-bit Architecture:**
  A 16-bit CPU can address **65,536 locations** (2^16), using **2 bytes** of data. It has more address space than 8-bit systems, allowing it to manage larger data sizes.
- **32-bit Architecture:**
  A 32-bit system can address **4 billion locations** (2^32), using **4 bytes** of data in a single operation. It can manage larger datasets, such as large arrays, integers, or complex data types, and is widely used in many modern CPUs.
- **64-bit Architecture:**
  A 64-bit system can theoretically address **18.4 billion billion locations** (2^64), allowing for **massive memory** access. This type of architecture allows the CPU to handle **8 bytes** of data in a single operation and is the standard in most modern computers.

## 2. Addressing Modes

There are various types of **addressing modes** that tell the CPU where to fetch data from in memory. These include:

- **Immediate Addressing**: The value is provided directly in the instruction. Example:

```assembly
mov ax, 5      ; Load the value 5 into register AX
```

- **Direct Addressing**: The instruction specifies a memory address where data is stored. Example:

```
assembly

mov ax, [1000h] ; Load the data at memory
address 1000h into AX
```

- **Indirect Addressing**: A register holds the memory address, and data is accessed indirectly through the register. Example:

```
assembly

mov ax, [bx]     ; Load data from memory address
stored in BX into AX
```

- **Indexed Addressing**: This mode uses an index (like SI or DI) to reference memory, allowing for array-like access. Example:

```
assembly

mov ax, [bx + si]   ; Access data at address BX
+ SI
```

Understanding these addressing modes helps you optimize data access and memory usage in low-level programming.

## 5.3 MANAGING DIFFERENT TYPES OF DATA STRUCTURES AT THE LOW LEVEL

At the low level, memory is typically managed manually. Understanding how to create, modify, and manage data structures like arrays, linked lists, and stacks is essential for writing efficient assembly code.

## 1. Arrays

Arrays are collections of elements stored in contiguous memory locations. In low-level programming, arrays are created by allocating a block of memory, and each element is accessed using an index.

For example, a simple array of 4 integers (assuming each integer is 4 bytes) might be represented as:

- Memory Address 0x1000: 0x00000001
- Memory Address 0x1004: 0x00000002
- Memory Address 0x1008: 0x00000003
- Memory Address 0x100C: 0x00000004

## 2. Linked Lists

A linked list is a collection of elements (nodes) where each node contains a data value and a reference (pointer) to the next node. Managing a linked list at the low level involves manipulating pointers and memory addresses directly.

For example, a linked list of integers might look like:

- Node 1: Data = 10, Next = 0x1004
- Node 2: Data = 20, Next = 0x1008
- Node 3: Data = 30, Next = 0x0000 (end of list)

To navigate through a linked list in assembly, you would load the memory address of each node into a register, access its data, and then move to the next node by following the "Next" pointer.

### 3. Stacks

A **stack** is a data structure that follows the **Last In, First Out (LIFO)** principle. Data is pushed onto the stack, and the most recent item pushed is the first one to be popped off.

The **stack pointer (SP)** keeps track of the top of the stack. In low-level programming, you manually push and pop values from the stack using the PUSH and POP instructions.

**Example of Stack Operations:**

```
assembly

push ax        ; Push the value in AX onto the stack
pop bx         ; Pop the top value into BX
```

### 4. Dynamic Memory Allocation

At the low level, managing dynamic memory allocation involves requesting memory from the operating system (using system calls or interrupts) and keeping track of memory usage manually. In more modern systems, this would be handled by the operating system, but in low-level programming, you must implement your own memory management system.

---

## 5.4 Hands-On Example: Implementing a Dynamic Memory Manager in Assembly

Now that we understand the importance of memory management and data structures, let's walk through a basic example of implementing a simple **dynamic memory manager** in assembly. This example will use basic operations like **malloc** (memory allocation) and **free** (deallocating memory), simulating what would happen in a higher-level language.

<u>**Example: Basic Dynamic Memory Manager**</u>

Here, we will allocate memory dynamically using the **heap**, a region of memory used for dynamic allocation, and implement a simple version of **malloc** and **free**.

### Step 1: Allocating Memory

In assembly, we can allocate memory using the operating system's system calls. For simplicity, we'll simulate the allocation of memory by reserving a block of memory in the **data section** and simulating dynamic allocation and freeing through a loop.

### Step 2: Freeing Memory

When freeing memory, we need to manually clear the values and release the memory, which would be managed by the operating system in higher-level languages. This process involves setting specific memory locations back to a default value or null pointer.

Here's a basic implementation that simulates dynamic memory allocation and deallocation:

```assembly

section .data
    heap_start db 100, 0, 0, 0  ; Simulate the start
of a heap with a 100-byte block

section .text
    global _start

_start:
```

```
    ; Simulate malloc by "allocating" memory (move
data into the heap region)
    mov esi, heap_start      ; Load the starting
address of the heap into ESI
    mov byte [esi], 42       ; Write a value to
simulate data allocation (memory reserved)

    ; Free memory (set value to zero to simulate
freeing)
    mov byte [esi], 0        ; Set the first byte to
zero, simulating a free

    ; Exit program
    mov eax, 1               ; System call for exit
    xor ebx, ebx            ; Exit with status 0
    int 0x80                ; Interrupt to execute
system call
```

### Step 3: Simulating Real-World Allocations

In a more advanced dynamic memory manager, you would implement a system that tracks memory blocks, handles fragmentation, and ensures memory is properly allocated and freed without memory leaks. For instance, a **free list** could be used to track available blocks of memory and handle fragmentation efficiently.

# Conclusion

This chapter covered the fundamental concepts of data representation and memory management in low-level programming. We explored how data is represented in binary and hexadecimal formats, the importance of memory addressing in different CPU architectures, and the techniques used to manage memory and data structures like arrays, linked lists, and stacks.

Through a hands-on example, we built a simple dynamic memory manager in assembly, simulating the allocation and deallocation of memory. This example, while basic, provides insight into how memory management works at the hardware level and lays the foundation for more advanced topics in systems programming.

# Chapter 6: The Role of the CPU: Understanding Registers and the ALU

## 6.1 THE ARCHITECTURE OF THE CPU

The **Central Processing Unit (CPU)** is the heart of any computer system. It's the component responsible for executing instructions from programs, carrying out arithmetic operations, and controlling data flow within the system. Understanding the architecture of the CPU is fundamental to writing efficient low-level code, as it allows you to optimize your programs to make full use of the available hardware.

### 1. Basic CPU Structure

The architecture of a CPU typically consists of the following components:

- **Control Unit (CU):**
  The control unit is responsible for fetching instructions from memory, decoding them, and directing the rest of the CPU to execute the instructions. It manages the overall operation of the CPU, coordinating with other components to ensure that tasks are carried out in the correct order.
- **Arithmetic Logic Unit (ALU):**
  The ALU performs all arithmetic and logical operations, such as addition, subtraction, multiplication, division, and comparisons. It's the part of the CPU that directly processes the data.

- **Registers:**
  Registers are small, fast storage locations within the CPU used to hold data temporarily while the CPU is executing instructions. They are the fastest form of storage in a computer, but they are limited in number and size.
- **Bus Interface Unit (BIU):**
  The BIU is responsible for managing the communication between the CPU and other components, including memory and I/O devices. It handles the reading and writing of data to and from memory.

## 2. The Fetch-Decode-Execute Cycle

The CPU follows a cycle known as **fetch-decode-execute** to process instructions. Here's a brief overview of each stage:

- **Fetch**: The CPU retrieves the instruction from memory. The address of the instruction is stored in the **program counter (PC)**, which keeps track of where the CPU is in the program.
- **Decode**: The fetched instruction is decoded by the control unit. The instruction is parsed to determine what action the CPU needs to perform (e.g., arithmetic, data transfer, or control flow).
- **Execute**: The ALU and other components perform the operation specified by the instruction. The result may be stored in a register or in memory, depending on the instruction.

The fetch-decode-execute cycle repeats as long as there are instructions to process.

## 6.2 Understanding the ALU (Arithmetic Logic Unit) and Its Role in Executing Instructions

The **Arithmetic Logic Unit (ALU)** is one of the most crucial components of the CPU. It performs all the arithmetic and logical operations required for program execution. Understanding the ALU's role is key to understanding how the CPU processes data and executes instructions.

### 1. Types of Operations Performed by the ALU

The ALU performs a wide variety of operations, broadly classified into two categories:

- **Arithmetic Operations**: These are operations that manipulate numerical data, such as:
    - **Addition**: Adding two numbers.
    - **Subtraction**: Subtracting one number from another.
    - **Multiplication**: Multiplying two numbers.
    - **Division**: Dividing one number by another.

    Example: In assembly, you might use the ADD instruction to perform addition:

    ```assembly

    add ax, bx  ; Adds the contents of BX to AX and
    stores the result in AX
    ```

- **Logical Operations**: These operations work with binary data and perform bitwise manipulations, such as:
    - **AND**: Performs a bitwise AND operation.
    - **OR**: Performs a bitwise OR operation.
    - **XOR**: Performs a bitwise XOR operation.
    - **NOT**: Performs a bitwise negation (inverts the bits).

Example: In assembly, you might use the AND instruction for a logical operation:

```assembly
assembly

and ax, bx  ; Performs bitwise AND on AX and
BX, stores result in AX
```

The ALU can also perform more complex operations, like **shifting** and **comparing** data, but the fundamental operations are arithmetic and logical.

## 2. Flags and Condition Codes in the ALU

The ALU sets various **flags** in the **flags register** based on the result of an operation. These flags provide essential information about the outcome of an operation and control the flow of the program.

- **Zero Flag (ZF)**: Set if the result of the operation is zero.
- **Carry Flag (CF)**: Set if there is a carry out of the most significant bit in an addition operation or a borrow in a subtraction.
- **Sign Flag (SF)**: Set if the result is negative (i.e., the most significant bit is set).
- **Overflow Flag (OF)**: Set if an arithmetic overflow occurs (when the result of an operation is too large for the register to hold).
- **Parity Flag (PF)**: Set if the number of set bits (1s) in the result is even.

For example:

```assembly
assembly

add ax, bx  ; Adds BX to AX, and updates flags based
on the result
```

These flags can be used in **conditional jumps** to alter the flow of execution based on the result of previous operations. For example, you can use the JZ (Jump if Zero) instruction to jump if the Zero Flag is set (i.e., the result of a previous operation was zero).

## 6.3 REGISTERS AND THEIR ROLE IN STORING DATA DURING EXECUTION

Registers are small, fast storage locations inside the CPU that temporarily hold data during execution. They play a critical role in the CPU's ability to perform tasks quickly because accessing data from a register is much faster than accessing data from memory.

### 1. Types of Registers

There are several types of registers in the CPU, each with a specific function:

- **General-Purpose Registers**: These registers are used to store temporary data that the CPU is working with. The most commonly used general-purpose registers in the x86 architecture include:
    - **AX (Accumulator Register)**: Used for arithmetic operations and logic operations.
    - **BX (Base Register)**: Often used to hold a memory address or offset.
    - **CX (Count Register)**: Used in looping and string operations.
    - **DX (Data Register)**: Used for input/output operations.
- **Index Registers**: These registers are used for addressing and pointing to memory locations. Examples include:
    - **SI (Source Index)**: Used in string operations.

- o **DI (Destination Index)**: Used in string operations.
- **Pointer Registers**: These registers store memory addresses, particularly in relation to stack operations:
  - o **SP (Stack Pointer)**: Points to the top of the stack.
  - o **BP (Base Pointer)**: Points to the base of the current stack frame.
- **Segment Registers**: These registers store the addresses of memory segments:
  - o **CS (Code Segment)**: Holds the address of the code segment.
  - o **DS (Data Segment)**: Holds the address of the data segment.
  - o **SS (Stack Segment)**: Holds the address of the stack segment.
  - o **ES (Extra Segment)**: Used for additional data storage in some cases.

## 2. Role of Registers in Program Execution

When the CPU executes a program, the registers hold data temporarily for processing. For example:

- **Fetching Instructions**: The program counter (PC) is stored in a register, which tells the CPU where to fetch the next instruction from memory.
- **Executing Instructions**: When performing arithmetic operations, the operands (the values to be added, subtracted, etc.) are typically loaded into registers, the operation is performed by the ALU, and the result is stored back into a register.

For example, adding two numbers could be done in the following steps:

assembly

```
mov ax, 5          ; Load the value 5 into register AX
```

```
mov bx, 10          ; Load the value 10 into register
BX
add ax, bx          ; Add the value of BX to AX, result
in AX (15)
```

Here, the values 5 and 10 are loaded into the AX and BX registers, respectively. The ADD instruction adds the contents of BX to AX, and the result (15) is stored in AX.

### 3. Importance of Register Usage

Efficient register usage is crucial for high-performance assembly programming. The CPU has a limited number of registers, so managing these registers effectively allows for faster program execution. In assembly, much of the work involves transferring data into and out of registers to perform operations quickly.

---

## 6.4 HANDS-ON EXAMPLE: WRITING ASSEMBLY CODE TO MANIPULATE CPU REGISTERS DIRECTLY

Now that we understand the basic architecture of the CPU, the ALU, and how registers work, let's dive into an example of writing assembly code that directly manipulates CPU registers.

We will create a simple program that:

1.  Loads values into registers.
2.  Performs arithmetic operations.
3.  Uses flags to control the program flow.
4.  Outputs the result.

## Example: Register Manipulation and Arithmetic Operations

In this example, we will:

1. Add two numbers.
2. Subtract two numbers.
3. Use flags to check the result of an operation and conditionally jump.

assembly

```assembly
section .data
    num1 db 10              ; First number
    num2 db 20              ; Second number

section .text
    global _start

_start:
    ; Load num1 into AX
    mov al, [num1]          ; Load first number into AL
    mov bl, [num2]          ; Load second number into BL

    ; Perform addition
    add al, bl              ; Add BL to AL, result in AL

    ; Compare AL and 0 (check if result is zero)
    cmp al, 0
    je zero_result          ; Jump to zero_result if AL
is zero

    ; Perform subtraction
    sub al, bl              ; Subtract BL from AL, result
in AL
    cmp al, 0
    jg positive_result      ; Jump to positive_result if
AL > 0
    jl negative_result      ; Jump to negative_result if
AL < 0

zero_result:
    ; Handle the case where result is zero
```

```
       mov eax, 1
       int 0x80                ; Exit program with status 1
positive_result:
       ; Handle the case where result is positive
       mov eax, 1
       int 0x80                ; Exit program with status 1
negative_result:
       ; Handle the case where result is negative
       mov eax, 1
       int 0x80                ; Exit program with status 1
```

In this code:

- We load values into registers AL and BL using the MOV instruction.
- We perform arithmetic operations (ADD, SUB) and use the CMP instruction to compare the result.
- We conditionally jump to different sections of code based on the flags set by the CMP instruction (Zero Flag, Greater Than, Less Than).

This example demonstrates how directly manipulating CPU registers can control the flow of the program and handle data efficiently.

---

## CONCLUSION

In this chapter, we've explored the architecture of the CPU, focusing on the role of the **ALU** and **registers**. We discussed the types of instructions the CPU executes, the importance of flags and condition codes in controlling program flow, and how to manipulate CPU registers directly in assembly.

Understanding these concepts is crucial for writing efficient low-level code. By working directly with the CPU's architecture, you can achieve highly optimized performance, especially for applications requiring low-latency processing, such as in embedded systems or real-time applications.

# Chapter 7: System Calls and Interfacing with the Operating System

## 7.1 WHAT ARE SYSTEM CALLS?

In the world of low-level systems programming, **system calls** are a key concept. A system call is a request made by a program to the operating system (OS) to perform a specific operation, such as reading from a file, allocating memory, or printing output to the screen. System calls provide an interface between user-level applications and the underlying hardware, allowing programs to interact with the operating system in a safe and controlled manner.

### 1. The Need for System Calls

Modern operating systems are designed to manage hardware resources efficiently and securely. Direct access to hardware is often restricted for user programs in order to maintain system stability and security. System calls act as an intermediary, allowing applications to request services from the OS without needing direct access to the hardware.

For example, when you want to read data from a file, a user-level program cannot directly interact with the storage hardware. Instead, the program makes a system call, asking the operating system to manage the file I/O operations on its behalf.

## 2. User Space vs. Kernel Space

To understand system calls, it's important to grasp the distinction between **user space** and **kernel space**:

- **User Space**: This is where user applications run. Programs in user space have limited access to system resources for security and stability reasons.
- **Kernel Space**: The kernel is the core part of the operating system, managing hardware resources such as memory, processors, and I/O devices. It operates with higher privileges than user space applications.

System calls provide a controlled entry point for user programs to request services from the kernel, such as reading or writing to a file, allocating memory, or interacting with hardware.

## 3. How System Calls Work

When a system call is invoked, the CPU switches from **user mode** to **kernel mode**, where it executes the requested operation with higher privileges. After the operation is completed, the CPU switches back to user mode and returns control to the user program. This transition is often referred to as a **context switch**.

In x86-based systems, system calls are typically invoked using software interrupts, such as **int 0x80** in Linux for 32-bit systems or the **syscall** instruction for 64-bit systems. The system call number (an integer) and any necessary arguments are passed via registers, and the operating system uses this information to perform the appropriate action.

## 7.2 How to Interface with an OS at a Low Level

Interfacing with the operating system at a low level involves making system calls, typically through assembly or C. While high-level languages provide abstracted methods for interacting with the OS, low-level programming requires you to directly invoke system calls and handle the underlying details yourself.

### 1. Understanding the Interface to the OS

When interacting with the OS through system calls, you need to understand the following components:

- **System Call Numbers**: Each system call is associated with a unique number that the OS uses to identify the requested service. For example, in Linux:
    - 1 corresponds to the `write` system call (for writing to a file or output).
    - 3 corresponds to the `read` system call (for reading from a file).

    These numbers are crucial for invoking system calls correctly.

- **Registers and Arguments**: Most system calls accept one or more arguments, such as memory addresses or file descriptors. These arguments are typically passed through CPU registers. For example:
    - For Linux system calls on x86, the **EBX** register often holds the first argument, **ECX** holds the second, and so on.
- **Return Values**: After a system call completes, the return value is usually stored in the **EAX** register (on x86 systems). If the operation was successful, this value may indicate the

result, such as the number of bytes read or written. If the operation failed, an error code (such as -1) may be returned.

## 2. Making a System Call in Assembly

To make a system call in assembly, you generally follow these steps:

1. Place the system call number in the appropriate register (e.g., EAX in x86).
2. Place any arguments for the system call in the corresponding registers (e.g., EBX, ECX).
3. Use the int 0x80 instruction (on x86 systems) or syscall instruction (on x86-64 systems) to trigger the system call.
4. After the system call executes, the return value can be retrieved from the EAX register (on x86 systems).

Here's an example of invoking the write system call on a Linux system:

```assembly
section .data
    msg db 'Hello, World!', 0xA  ; Message to be written to stdout
    msg_len equ $-msg            ; Length of the message

section .text
    global _start

_start:
    ; Write the message to stdout (file descriptor 1)
    mov eax, 4              ; System call number for 'write'
    mov ebx, 1             ; File descriptor 1 (stdout)
    mov ecx, msg          ; Pointer to the message
    mov edx, msg_len      ; Length of the message
    int 0x80              ; Invoke system call
```

```
; Exit the program
    mov eax, 1                  ; System call number for
'exit'
    xor ebx, ebx                ; Exit status 0
    int 0x80                    ; Invoke system call
```

In this example:

- EAX is set to 4 to indicate the `write` system call.
- EBX is set to 1 for the `stdout` file descriptor.
- ECX holds the address of the message, and EDX holds the length of the message.
- The `int 0x80` instruction triggers the system call.

## 3. Interfacing with the OS Using C

In higher-level languages like C, interfacing with the OS is simpler and more abstracted. For example, using the `write` system call in C looks like this:

c

```c
#include <unistd.h>

int main() {
    const char *msg = "Hello, World!\n";
    write(1, msg, 14);   // File descriptor 1 is
stdout
    return 0;
}
```

The `write` function in C internally invokes the corresponding system call, handling the low-level details for you.

## 7.3 THE ROLE OF THE OPERATING SYSTEM IN MANAGING RESOURCES

The operating system plays a critical role in managing the system's resources, ensuring that hardware and software work together efficiently and securely. Here are the primary resources managed by the OS:

### 1. Memory Management

Memory management is one of the core responsibilities of the operating system. It involves allocating, tracking, and deallocating memory for running programs. This ensures that programs have enough memory to operate without interfering with each other. The OS provides services like:

- **Memory Allocation**: The OS allocates memory to programs, including the stack, heap, and data segments.
- **Virtual Memory**: Virtual memory allows programs to use more memory than is physically available by swapping data in and out of disk storage.
- **Memory Protection**: The OS ensures that programs cannot access or modify memory regions allocated to other programs, protecting against memory corruption and security vulnerabilities.

### 2. Input/Output (I/O) Management

The OS manages all I/O operations, including reading from and writing to devices like hard drives, keyboards, and network interfaces. I/O management involves:

- **Device Drivers**: These are programs that allow the OS to interact with hardware devices. For example, a device driver may allow the OS to read data from a disk or send data to a printer.

- **File System**: The OS provides a file system for organizing, storing, and accessing files. It abstracts away the underlying hardware so that programs can read and write files without needing to understand the specifics of the storage device.

## 3. Process Management

The OS manages the execution of processes, which are running instances of programs. It handles tasks like:

- **Process Scheduling**: The OS schedules which process should run at any given time, ensuring that each process gets CPU time.
- **Context Switching**: When switching between processes, the OS saves the state of the current process and loads the state of the next process.
- **Synchronization**: The OS ensures that processes cooperate efficiently, especially when they share resources like memory or I/O devices.

---

## 7.4 HANDS-ON EXAMPLE: WRITING A PROGRAM THAT INTERACTS WITH THE OS TO READ AND WRITE FILES

Let's walk through a hands-on example where we create a program that interacts with the operating system to read from a file and write to another file. This will involve using system calls directly in assembly.

## Example: Reading and Writing Files Using System Calls

This program will:

1. Open a file for reading.
2. Read its contents into memory.
3. Write the contents to a new file.

```assembly
section .data
    input_file db 'input.txt', 0    ; Name of the
input file
    output_file db 'output.txt', 0  ; Name of the
output file
    buffer resb 100                 ; Reserve 100
bytes for the buffer

section .text
    global _start

_start:
    ; Open the input file (read-only mode)
    mov eax, 5              ; System call number for
'open'
    mov ebx, input_file    ; Pointer to the input file
name
    mov ecx, 0             ; Read-only flag (O_RDONLY)
    int 0x80              ; Invoke the system call

    mov ebx, eax          ; File descriptor of the
input file

    ; Read from the input file
    mov eax, 3             ; System call number for
'read'
    mov ecx, buffer       ; Pointer to the buffer
    mov edx, 100          ; Number of bytes to read
    int 0x80             ; Invoke the system call

    ; Open the output file (create if not exists)
```

```
    mov eax, 5              ; System call number for
'open'
    mov ebx, output_file    ; Pointer to the output
file name
    mov ecx, 577            ; Flags for O_WRONLY |
O_CREAT | O_TRUNC
    mov edx, 0644o          ; File permissions (rw-r--
r--)
    int 0x80                ; Invoke the system call

    mov ebx, eax            ; File descriptor of the
output file

    ; Write the data to the output file
    mov eax, 4              ; System call number for
'write'
    mov ecx, buffer         ; Pointer to the buffer
    mov edx, 100            ; Number of bytes to write
    int 0x80                ; Invoke the system call

    ; Exit the program
    mov eax, 1              ; System call number for
'exit'
    xor ebx, ebx            ; Exit status 0
    int 0x80                ; Invoke the system call
```

## Step-by-Step Explanation:

1. **Opening Files**:
   - We use the open system call to open the input file
     (input.txt) for reading and the output file
     (output.txt) for writing.
   - The file descriptor for each file is returned in the EAX
     register, and we store it in the EBX register for further
     use.
2. **Reading Data**:
   - The read system call is invoked to read up to 100
     bytes from the input file into a buffer.
3. **Writing Data**:
   - The write system call is used to write the contents
     of the buffer to the output file.
4. **Exiting**:

o Finally, the `exit` system call is invoked to terminate the program.

---

## CONCLUSION

In this chapter, we've explored the fundamental concept of system calls and how they allow programs to interact with the operating system. We learned about the different types of system calls, how they are invoked, and how the OS manages system resources like memory, I/O, and processes.

Through a hands-on example, we demonstrated how to use system calls to read from one file and write to another, giving a practical example of low-level programming and OS interaction.

Understanding system calls is critical for any low-level programmer, as they form the foundation for communicating with the operating system and leveraging its services effectively.

# Chapter 8: Optimizing Assembly Code for Performance

## 8.1 How to Write Highly Efficient Assembly Code

Assembly language provides the developer with direct control over the CPU, allowing for highly optimized and performance-critical code. However, writing efficient assembly code requires a deep understanding of the CPU's inner workings, memory management, and the specific instructions available for your processor. Optimizing assembly code for performance isn't just about making the code shorter or faster—it's about writing code that efficiently utilizes the system's resources while maintaining clarity and correctness.

### 1. Understanding CPU Architecture for Optimization

The first step in optimizing assembly code is understanding the specific CPU architecture you're working with. Different processors (x86, ARM, etc.) have distinct instruction sets, register sizes, and performance characteristics. Therefore, the optimizations you apply to your code will vary depending on the architecture.

- **Registers and Cache**: Registers are the fastest form of memory, and accessing them is much quicker than accessing memory. Cache memory, which stores frequently accessed data, is also faster than main memory. Optimizing code to make use of registers and reduce cache misses can significantly improve performance.

- **Pipelining and Parallelism**: Modern CPUs use **instruction pipelining**, allowing them to process multiple instructions simultaneously. Efficient assembly code takes advantage of this by structuring operations in such a way that multiple instructions can be processed in parallel, minimizing idle CPU time.

## 2. Efficient Use of Registers

Registers are the CPU's primary resource for storing data temporarily. Since registers are fast and directly accessible, maximizing their usage is a key optimization strategy. Here are some tips for working with registers efficiently:

- **Minimize Memory Access**: The more frequently you access memory, the slower your code will be. Instead, load values into registers and operate on them directly. After performing calculations, store the result back in memory only when necessary.
- **Choose the Right Registers**: Modern processors have multiple types of registers (general-purpose, index, and pointer registers). Use them strategically to hold values that are frequently accessed during execution.
- **Avoid Register Spilling**: If there aren't enough registers to hold all necessary data, the system may need to spill data to the stack. This is a slow operation, so aim to minimize register spilling by using registers efficiently and reducing the number of variables you store.

## 3. Optimizing Instructions

Assembly code is essentially a sequence of instructions that manipulate data. Understanding how to optimize these instructions can have a major impact on performance.

- **Choose Instructions Carefully**: Not all instructions are equal. Some instructions, like multiplication or division, are slower than others (e.g., addition and subtraction). Whenever possible, replace slower operations with faster alternatives. For example, if you need to multiply by a power of 2, use a **shift** operation (`shl` or `shr`) instead of the `mul` instruction.
- **Avoid Unnecessary Operations**: Each instruction takes time to execute. Avoid performing redundant or unnecessary operations, such as repeatedly loading the same value into a register when it hasn't changed.
- **Use Efficient Branching**: Branching (i.e., jumping between sections of code) can slow down performance if not handled efficiently. Modern CPUs use **branch prediction** to anticipate which path the program will take, but unpredictable branches can still cause delays. Minimize branching where possible, and try to structure your code so that branches are predictable.

## 4. Pipeline Optimization

Modern CPUs employ pipelining to allow multiple instructions to be processed at once. To take advantage of pipelining, structure your assembly code so that the CPU can execute multiple instructions simultaneously without waiting for one to finish before starting the next.

- **Instruction Reordering**: Arrange instructions so that one instruction can execute while another is waiting for data. For example, if an instruction depends on a value that is being computed by a previous instruction, you can insert independent operations between them, allowing the CPU to process other instructions during the wait.
- **Avoid Data Hazards**: Data hazards occur when instructions depend on the result of previous instructions. There are three types of data hazards: read-after-write (RAW), write-

after-read (WAR), and write-after-write (WAW). By carefully ordering instructions and minimizing dependencies, you can avoid stalling the pipeline.

## 8.2 COMMON PERFORMANCE PITFALLS IN ASSEMBLY PROGRAMMING AND HOW TO AVOID THEM

While assembly language provides the tools for highly efficient code, there are several common performance pitfalls that programmers should watch out for. These mistakes can lead to inefficient code that runs slower than necessary. Below are some common performance pitfalls in assembly and how to avoid them.

### 1. Excessive Memory Access

One of the biggest performance bottlenecks in assembly programming is excessive memory access. Modern CPUs can access data from registers in nanoseconds, but accessing data from main memory can take hundreds of CPU cycles. Here are a few strategies to minimize memory access:

- **Store frequently used values in registers**: By keeping commonly used values in registers, you avoid the time cost of accessing memory. This is particularly useful for loop variables and frequently accessed data.
- **Use Local Variables**: If your program uses global variables, the CPU has to perform more complex memory lookups. Try to use local variables that are stored in the stack or registers, reducing the need to access global memory.

## 2. Overuse of Branching

Branching is a powerful tool, but excessive use of **conditional jumps** (`jmp`, `je`, `jne`, etc.) can disrupt CPU pipelining and slow down your program.

- **Minimize Branches**: If possible, try to replace conditional branches with arithmetic or logical operations. For example, instead of checking if a number is greater than 0, you can simply subtract it and check the result.
- **Optimize Loops**: In loops, try to reduce the number of branches inside the loop body. If the loop is highly dependent on branches, the CPU might need to re-fetch instructions frequently, which causes a performance hit.

## 3. Inefficient Looping

Loops are fundamental in almost every program, but poor loop design can significantly degrade performance. Here are a few tips to optimize loops:

- **Unroll Loops**: Loop unrolling is the process of expanding a loop to reduce the overhead of the loop control. For example, instead of iterating over an array one element at a time, you could process multiple elements in a single loop iteration. This reduces the overhead of checking loop conditions and updating the loop counter.
- **Avoid Redundant Calculations in Loops**: Repeatedly calculating the same value inside a loop (such as an address or a constant) wastes time. Compute these values once before the loop starts and reuse them.

### 4. Improper Use of Registers

Overusing registers can also lead to inefficiency. While registers are fast, there's a limit to how many the CPU has, and overusing them can lead to performance degradation.

- **Balance Register Usage**: Use registers efficiently, but avoid using too many at once. If you run out of registers, the CPU may have to use memory, which is slower.
- **Stack Management**: If you use the stack to save values, ensure that you pop values off the stack in the correct order. Unnecessary push and pop operations can slow down execution.

---

## 8.3 USING LOOPS AND FUNCTIONS EFFICIENTLY IN LOW-LEVEL PROGRAMMING

In low-level assembly programming, loops and functions play a vital role in structuring code. Efficient use of loops and functions is crucial for optimizing performance.

### 1. Loop Optimization

When writing loops in assembly, it's essential to minimize the overhead of the loop structure itself. Here are a few strategies to optimize loops:

- **Loop Unrolling**: As mentioned earlier, loop unrolling reduces the number of iterations in a loop by processing multiple elements in a single pass.

Example of loop unrolling:

```assembly
assembly

; Original loop
loop:
    mov ax, [bx]
    add ax, [bx+2]
    inc bx
    dec cx
    jnz loop

; Unrolled loop (for two elements at a time)
unrolled_loop:
    mov ax, [bx]
    add ax, [bx+2]
    mov dx, [bx+4]
    add dx, [bx+6]
    inc bx
    dec cx
    jnz unrolled_loop
```

- **Minimize Loop Condition Checks**: Avoid checking the loop condition more often than necessary. For example, you can calculate the loop condition once before the loop starts, rather than recalculating it on each iteration.

## 2. Efficient Function Calls

Functions (or subroutines) are essential for breaking code into manageable pieces, but calling functions involves overhead. In assembly, you need to consider the cost of pushing arguments to the stack and jumping to the function.

- **Minimize Function Calls**: If a function is small and called frequently, consider inlining it directly into the caller to avoid the overhead of a function call.
- **Pass Arguments via Registers**: Instead of pushing function arguments to the stack, use registers to pass arguments. This reduces the time spent manipulating the stack.

- **Return Early**: If a function has multiple return conditions, try to return as early as possible to minimize unnecessary computation.

---

## 8.4 HANDS-ON EXAMPLE: OPTIMIZING A SORTING ALGORITHM IN ASSEMBLY

Sorting algorithms are an excellent example of how to optimize assembly code. In this example, we will take a simple **bubble sort** algorithm and optimize it to improve its performance.

### Step 1: Basic Bubble Sort Implementation

Here's an unoptimized bubble sort in assembly. This simple algorithm repeatedly swaps adjacent elements if they are in the wrong order.

```assembly
section .data
    arr db 5, 3, 8, 1, 2      ; Array of integers to
sort
    arr_len equ $-arr         ; Length of the array

section .text
    global _start

_start:
    ; Initialize variables
    mov ecx, arr_len          ; Set loop counter to
length of array
    dec ecx                   ; Decrement by 1 to
avoid going out of bounds

bubble_sort:
```

```asm
    mov ebx, 0                  ; Set the index for
inner loop
    mov edx, ecx                ; Store the loop counter
in edx

inner_loop:
    mov al, [arr + ebx]         ; Load the current
element
    mov bl, [arr + ebx + 1]     ; Load the next element

    ; Compare the two elements and swap if necessary
    cmp al, bl
    jg swap_elements

    ; Move to the next pair
    inc ebx
    loop inner_loop
    dec ecx                     ; Decrement outer loop
counter
    jnz bubble_sort
    jmp done

swap_elements:
    ; Swap the elements
    mov [arr + ebx], bl
    mov [arr + ebx + 1], al
    inc ebx
    jmp inner_loop

done:
    ; Exit program
    mov eax, 1                  ; System call number for
'exit'
    xor ebx, ebx                ; Exit status 0
    int 0x80                    ; Invoke system call
```

### Step 2: Optimizing the Bubble Sort

The main optimization here is reducing the number of unnecessary comparisons. In a standard bubble sort, each iteration checks all pairs of elements, even if no swaps were made in the previous iteration. This results in redundant work.

One common optimization is to **track whether any swaps were made** during the pass. If no swaps occur, the array is already sorted, and we can exit early.

Here's an optimized version of the bubble sort:

```assembly
section .data
    arr db 5, 3, 8, 1, 2      ; Array of integers to sort
    arr_len equ $-arr          ; Length of the array

section .text
    global _start

_start:
    ; Initialize variables
    mov ecx, arr_len           ; Set loop counter to length of array
    dec ecx                    ; Decrement by 1 to avoid going out of bounds

bubble_sort:
    mov ebx, 0                 ; Set the index for inner loop
    mov edx, ecx               ; Store the loop counter in edx
    mov esi, 0                 ; Flag to track swaps

inner_loop:
    mov al, [arr + ebx]        ; Load the current element
    mov bl, [arr + ebx + 1]    ; Load the next element

    ; Compare the two elements and swap if necessary
    cmp al, bl
    jg swap_elements

    ; Move to the next pair
    inc ebx
    loop inner_loop
```

```
    ; If no swaps were made, break the loop early
    cmp esi, 0
    je done
    dec ecx                     ; Decrement outer loop
counter
    jnz bubble_sort

done:
    ; Exit program
    mov eax, 1                  ; System call number for
'exit'
    xor ebx, ebx                ; Exit status 0
    int 0x80                    ; Invoke system call

swap_elements:
    ; Swap the elements
    mov [arr + ebx], bl
    mov [arr + ebx + 1], al
    mov esi, 1                  ; Set swap flag
    inc ebx
    jmp inner_loop
```
**Step 3: Further Optimizations**

The optimized bubble sort now exits early if no swaps are made in a pass. However, there are additional optimizations you can make:

- **Loop unrolling**: Reducing the overhead of looping by processing multiple elements in one iteration.
- **Using a more efficient sorting algorithm**: Bubble sort is inherently inefficient. Optimizing your sorting algorithm (e.g., using **quick sort** or **merge sort**) can provide much better performance for large datasets.

## CONCLUSION

In this chapter, we've covered how to write highly efficient assembly code by focusing on register usage, minimizing memory access, and optimizing instruction sequences. We also identified common performance pitfalls in assembly programming and strategies to avoid them.

We discussed the importance of loops and functions in low-level programming and demonstrated how optimizing these structures can lead to significant performance improvements. Through the hands-on example of optimizing a bubble sort algorithm, we explored how small changes can make a big difference in execution time.

# Chapter 9: Error Handling and Debugging in Low-Level Systems

## 9.1 COMMON ERRORS IN LOW-LEVEL PROGRAMMING

Low-level programming, especially in languages like assembly, comes with unique challenges. Since assembly language works directly with the hardware, a single mistake can lead to catastrophic errors, such as system crashes, data corruption, or unpredictable behavior. Understanding and recognizing common errors is the first step in effectively debugging and optimizing low-level code.

### 1. Syntax Errors

In any programming language, **syntax errors** are among the most common. These errors occur when the program violates the rules of the language's syntax, making it impossible for the assembler (or compiler) to translate the source code into machine code. While high-level languages tend to offer more helpful error messages for syntax errors, assembly language requires a keen understanding of the instruction set and conventions.

**Examples of Syntax Errors:**

- **Missing operands**: Some instructions require two operands (e.g., MOV), and missing one can cause a syntax error.

  ```assembly
  assembly

  mov ax, ; Error: Missing operand
  ```

- **Invalid labels**: Labels in assembly must follow specific rules, such as starting with a letter and containing only alphanumeric characters and underscores.

  ```assembly
  1_start: ; Error: Label name cannot start with a number
  ```

- **Misplaced directives**: Certain assembly directives, such as `.data` and `.text`, must appear in the correct order. Placing a `.data` section after the `.text` section can lead to errors.

To fix these errors, carefully review the syntax rules of the assembler you're using and ensure all instructions, labels, and directives are correctly formatted.

## 2. Segmentation Faults (Access Violations)

One of the most frustrating errors when dealing with low-level programming is a **segmentation fault**. This occurs when a program attempts to access memory that it is not permitted to access, such as reading from or writing to memory that hasn't been allocated or trying to dereference a null or invalid pointer.

In assembly, segmentation faults can occur for several reasons:

- **Accessing uninitialized memory**: Trying to read or write data to a memory location that hasn't been allocated.
- **Pointer errors**: Dereferencing a pointer that points to an invalid or unallocated memory location.
- **Stack overflow**: Recursively calling functions without proper limits or overwriting the stack, causing the program to access memory beyond its allocated space.

### 3. Memory Leaks

Memory leaks occur when a program allocates memory but fails to free it after use. Over time, memory leaks can accumulate, leading to increased memory consumption and, eventually, system instability or crashes.

In low-level programming, managing memory manually is crucial. Unlike higher-level languages, which often have garbage collection to manage memory automatically, assembly requires explicit management. Memory leaks can happen if:

- **Memory allocated with `malloc` (or similar system calls) is never freed.**
- **Memory used by the program is overwritten or lost without being properly deallocated.**

To avoid memory leaks, always ensure that each dynamically allocated memory block is properly deallocated when it is no longer needed. Use careful tracking of memory allocation and deallocation operations.

## 9.2 USING DEBUGGERS AND OTHER TOOLS FOR TROUBLESHOOTING

Debugging assembly code can be tricky, especially since errors might not manifest in the usual way. Using debuggers and other tools can help identify, isolate, and fix issues in your low-level programs.

# 1. What is a Debugger?

A **debugger** is a tool that allows you to inspect and control the execution of a program. It provides functionality to:

- Set breakpoints: Pause the program at a specific point in execution.
- Step through code: Execute one instruction at a time, allowing you to see the program's state at each step.
- Examine registers and memory: View the contents of registers, memory, and the stack to understand the program's behavior.

In assembly language, debuggers are essential for inspecting the state of the CPU, registers, and memory as the program runs. A debugger can help identify exactly where a program is crashing, reading from uninitialized memory, or causing other issues.

## 2. Using GDB (GNU Debugger)

For Linux-based systems, **GDB** is a powerful and widely-used debugger that allows you to step through assembly code and inspect various aspects of the program's execution. GDB can be used to debug programs written in assembly, C, and other languages.

Here's a basic workflow for using GDB to debug an assembly program:

1. **Compile your assembly program with debugging symbols**: Use the -g flag with your assembler to include debugging symbols in the output.

   bash

```
nasm -f elf64 -g -F dwarf program.asm -o
program.o
ld -o program program.o
```

2. **Start GDB**: Launch GDB with the compiled program:

```bash
gdb ./program
```

3. **Set breakpoints**: In GDB, you can set breakpoints to pause the program at specific points.

```bash
break _start   ; Set a breakpoint at the
program's entry point
```

4. **Step through code**: Use the step command to execute the program one instruction at a time and examine the state of the program after each step.

```bash
step
```

5. **Inspect registers**: You can inspect the values of registers to understand how the program is manipulating data.

```bash
info registers   ; Display the contents of the
CPU registers
```

6. **Check memory**: Use GDB's memory inspection commands to examine specific memory addresses.

```bash
```

```
x/4x 0x1000   ; Examine 4 hexadecimal words
starting from address 0x1000
```

7.  **Exit GDB**: After debugging, you can exit GDB using the `quit` command:

```bash
```

```
quit
```

### 3. Using Other Tools

While debuggers like GDB are essential, other tools can assist in troubleshooting assembly code:

- **Valgrind**: This tool is useful for detecting memory leaks and memory management errors. It can be particularly helpful in catching errors related to dynamic memory allocation.
- **Strace**: For programs that interact with the operating system, `strace` can be used to trace system calls and signals, allowing you to monitor file I/O, memory allocation, and other interactions.

## 9.3 HOW TO HANDLE EXCEPTIONS AND ERRORS IN ASSEMBLY CODE

Handling errors in assembly language is a critical aspect of writing reliable programs. While higher-level languages provide built-in exception handling, assembly requires a more manual approach. Here's how you can handle errors and exceptions in low-level assembly code.

## 1. Using System Calls for Error Handling

System calls often return error codes when something goes wrong. For instance, when attempting to open a file, the `open` system call will return -1 if the file cannot be opened. Similarly, the `read` and `write` system calls return the number of bytes read or written, and if an error occurs, they return -1.

To handle errors, you should always check the return value of system calls and take appropriate action. Here's an example of error handling after trying to open a file:

```assembly
mov eax, 5           ; System call number for 'open'
mov ebx, file_name   ; File name to open
mov ecx, 0           ; Read-only flag
int 0x80             ; Invoke the system call

cmp eax, -1          ; Check if the file was opened
successfully
je error_opening_file ; Jump to error handling if eax
= -1

; Normal program flow if no error occurs

error_opening_file:
    ; Handle the error, such as printing a message
    mov eax, 4       ; System call number for
'write'
    mov ebx, 1       ; File descriptor 1 (stdout)
    mov ecx, error_msg ; Error message address
    mov edx, error_len ; Error message length
    int 0x80         ; Invoke system call to display
the error
    mov eax, 1       ; System call number for 'exit'
    xor ebx, ebx     ; Exit status 0
    int 0x80         ; Invoke system call to exit
```

In this example, the program checks the return value of the open system call. If the return value is -1, the program jumps to the error handling section, where an error message is printed.

### 2. Exception Handling in Assembly

While assembly does not provide a built-in mechanism for handling exceptions like higher-level languages, you can design a simple error-handling mechanism by using **interrupts** or **trap handlers**. For example, if a certain operation might cause an overflow or invalid memory access, you can use system calls to safely handle such errors.

### 3. Clean Up and Exit Gracefully

Always ensure that your program exits gracefully, even if an error occurs. This means:

- Freeing any allocated resources.
- Closing any open files.
- Restoring the system to a stable state.

In assembly, you'll need to manually handle these tasks. For example, if your program allocates memory using system calls, make sure to free the memory when done, even if an error occurs.

---

## 9.4 HANDS-ON EXAMPLE: DEBUGGING A SIMPLE ASSEMBLY PROGRAM WITH COMMON ERRORS

Let's put the concepts we've learned into practice. In this hands-on example, we will write a simple assembly program with intentional errors, debug it using GDB, and fix the issues.

## Step 1: Write the Program with Errors

Here's a simple program that attempts to add two numbers and print the result. We'll introduce some errors that we'll debug later.

```assembly
section .data
    num1 db 10          ; First number
    num2 db 20          ; Second number
    result db 0         ; Result placeholder

section .text
    global _start

_start:
    mov al, [num1]      ; Load num1 into AL
    add al, [num2]      ; Add num2 to AL
    mov [result], al    ; Store the result in the
result variable

    ; Print the result (Error: no valid system call
for printing single byte)
    mov eax, 4          ; System call number for
'write'
    mov ebx, 1          ; File descriptor 1 (stdout)
    mov ecx, result     ; Pointer to the result
    mov edx, 1          ; Length of the result (1 byte)
    int 0x80            ; Invoke system call

    ; Exit program
    mov eax, 1          ; System call number for 'exit'
    xor ebx, ebx        ; Exit status 0
    int 0x80            ; Invoke system call
```

In this code:

- There is an issue with printing the result. The `write` system call expects a pointer to a string or data larger than 1 byte (or properly formatted for display). This will result in a crash when trying to print the result.

## Step 2: Use GDB to Debug

Compile the code with debugging symbols and run it in GDB to debug.

1. **Compile with Debugging Symbols**:

   bash

   ```
   nasm -f elf64 -g -F dwarf program.asm -o
   program.o
   ld -s -o program program.o
   ```

2. **Start GDB**:

   bash

   ```
   gdb ./program
   ```

3. **Set Breakpoints and Step Through Code**: Set a breakpoint at _start and step through the program line by line.

   bash

   ```
   break _start
   run
   step
   ```

4. **Inspect Registers and Memory**: Use GDB to inspect the contents of registers and memory. Check whether the AL register holds the expected sum of the two numbers.

   bash

   ```
   info registers
   x/1xb $result
   ```

5. **Fix the Error**: Once you identify the issue with printing the result, update the program to correctly handle the output

(e.g., converting the number to a string format or using a larger memory buffer to hold the result).

## CONCLUSION

In this chapter, we've explored the common errors encountered in low-level systems programming, such as syntax errors, segmentation faults, and memory leaks. We also learned how to use debuggers like GDB to troubleshoot and fix issues in assembly programs. Additionally, we covered the importance of handling exceptions and ensuring that the program exits gracefully.

Through a hands-on example, we demonstrated how to debug a simple assembly program, identify errors, and implement solutions to fix them. Debugging is an essential skill for any low-level programmer, and mastering tools like GDB will help you efficiently troubleshoot and optimize your assembly programs.

# Chapter 10: Interfacing with External Hardware: Input/Output and Beyond

## 10.1 The Basics of I/O Ports and How Low-Level Programs Interact with External Hardware

In low-level systems programming, one of the most powerful aspects is the ability to interface with external hardware directly. The CPU and memory aren't isolated; they communicate with the outside world through **input/output (I/O)** ports. These ports act as communication channels between the computer and external devices like keyboards, displays, sensors, and even motors. Low-level programs are responsible for managing this interaction efficiently, enabling precise control over the hardware.

### 1. What are I/O Ports?

I/O ports are specific memory addresses that the CPU uses to communicate with hardware. They can be thought of as doorways through which data flows between the processor and external devices. These ports can either be **data ports** (for transferring data) or **control ports** (for sending commands to a device).

In **x86 systems**, I/O ports are typically addressed using **inb, outb, inw**, and **outw** instructions, which correspond to input and output operations for bytes (8 bits) or words (16 bits). For example:

- **inb**: Read a byte of data from an I/O port.
- **outb**: Write a byte of data to an I/O port.

Here's an example of using I/O ports in assembly language:

```assembly
mov al, 0x01     ; Load the value to be written
(0x01) into register AL
out 0x60, al     ; Output the value of AL to I/O port
0x60
```

## 2. Types of I/O Ports

I/O ports come in different forms, depending on the system's architecture and how the hardware is designed to communicate with the CPU:

- **Memory-Mapped I/O (MMIO)**: In this model, devices are treated as if they were part of the system's memory. Instead of accessing a specific I/O port, the CPU directly accesses specific memory addresses to communicate with devices.
- **Port-Mapped I/O (PMIO)**: Here, devices are accessed via specific I/O ports that are separate from the main memory. These ports are typically mapped to a range of addresses within the CPU's address space.

The method of access—whether memory-mapped or port-mapped—depends on the architecture and design of the hardware.

## 3. I/O Operations

The **read** and **write** operations are the fundamental methods of interacting with external devices. These operations can involve either single-byte transfers or multi-byte transfers, depending on the device and the protocol being used. For instance, simple I/O devices like keyboards or LEDs often use byte-sized operations, while more complex devices like sensors or network interfaces might require word or double-word operations.

Each I/O device typically has a **control register**, which is used to send commands or configurations to the device. For example, writing a specific value to a control register can turn a device on or off or configure it for a particular operation.

## 10.2 UNDERSTANDING SERIAL COMMUNICATION PROTOCOLS

When interacting with external hardware, especially embedded devices, understanding **serial communication protocols** is essential. These protocols define how data is transferred between devices over short or long distances. Serial communication sends data one bit at a time, making it an efficient method for transmitting data over long distances or between devices with limited resources.

### 1. Universal Asynchronous Receiver/Transmitter (UART)

UART is one of the simplest and most widely used serial communication protocols. It allows two devices to communicate by sending data one bit at a time, with each device using a UART module to convert between parallel and serial data.

- **How UART Works**: UART communication typically uses two wires:
    - **TX (Transmit)**: Sends data from the transmitting device.
    - **RX (Receive)**: Receives data on the receiving device.

Data is transmitted in **frames**, each containing a start bit, data bits, an optional parity bit, and a stop bit. The frame structure ensures that both devices can synchronize and interpret the transmitted data correctly.

- **Example Use Case**: UART is commonly used in microcontroller communication, such as sending data to a serial console or communicating with GPS modules.

**Sending Data via UART**: To send data over UART, you write to the UART transmit register (usually mapped to a specific I/O port). Here's an example in assembly where the character 'A' is sent through a UART interface:

```assembly
mov al, 'A'          ; Load the ASCII value for 'A'
out 0x3F8, al        ; Write the value to the UART
transmit port (0x3F8)
```

## 2. Serial Peripheral Interface (SPI)

SPI is a more complex but faster protocol than UART, designed for high-speed data exchange between microcontrollers and peripheral devices. It is commonly used for communication with sensors, displays, and memory chips. SPI uses four wires:

- **MISO (Master In Slave Out)**: The line that carries data from the slave to the master.
- **MOSI (Master Out Slave In)**: The line that carries data from the master to the slave.
- **SCK (Serial Clock)**: The clock signal generated by the master to synchronize communication.
- **SS (Slave Select)**: A signal used by the master to select which slave device it wants to communicate with.
- **How SPI Works**: Data is shifted into the receiving device on each clock cycle, and the master device controls the clock

signal. SPI is often used in situations where high-speed, full-duplex communication is required.

**Example of SPI Communication:**

```
assembly

mov al, 0xFF        ; Load the data to send
out 0x4000, al      ; Send the data via SPI (0x4000
is a hypothetical SPI port)
```

### 3. Inter-Integrated Circuit (I2C)

I2C is a two-wire protocol used for communication between a master and one or more slave devices. It is widely used in sensors, EEPROMs, and real-time clocks. The two wires used in I2C are:

- **SDA (Serial Data):** Used to transmit and receive data.
- **SCL (Serial Clock):** Carries the clock signal for synchronization.

I2C supports multiple devices on the same bus, and each device has a unique address. It is slower than SPI but more flexible, as it allows multiple devices to share the same communication lines.

**Example of I2C Communication:** In assembly, sending data over I2C requires handling start conditions, address transmission, and data transfer in accordance with the protocol. Here's a simplified representation:

```
assembly

; Set up I2C transaction, send address and data
(simplified for illustration)
```

# 10.3 HANDS-ON EXAMPLE: WRITING A SIMPLE PROGRAM TO INTERFACE WITH AN EXTERNAL DEVICE (E.G., LED, MOTOR, OR SENSOR)

To make the concepts discussed more tangible, let's write a simple program that interacts with an external device. In this case, we will control an **LED** using a microcontroller, demonstrating how to send commands and data to a hardware device using low-level assembly code.

## Example: Blinking an LED Using UART Communication

We will create an assembly program for a microcontroller that uses the UART protocol to send data to an LED. When a specific command is received via UART, the LED will blink.

### Step 1: Set Up UART for Communication

Before communicating with the LED, we need to initialize the UART interface for serial communication. This involves configuring the baud rate, parity bits, and stop bits.

assembly

```
; Set baud rate to 9600
mov al, 0x0C    ; Baud rate divisor (9600 baud)
out 0x3F8, al   ; Send the baud rate divisor to UART
register
```

### Step 2: Sending Data to Control the LED

Next, we send a command to turn the LED on or off. For simplicity, let's assume that sending '1' will turn the LED on, and sending '0' will turn it off.

assembly

```assembly
; Send '1' to turn on the LED
mov al, '1'      ; Load the data to send (turn on
LED)
out 0x3F8, al    ; Send the data via UART
```

**Step 3: Blinking the LED**

To make the LED blink, we will implement a simple loop that repeatedly turns the LED on and off with a short delay.

```assembly
assembly

blink_led:
    mov al, '1'      ; Turn on the LED
    out 0x3F8, al    ; Send command to UART to turn
on LED
    call delay       ; Wait for a short period

    mov al, '0'      ; Turn off the LED
    out 0x3F8, al    ; Send command to UART to turn
off LED
    call delay       ; Wait for a short period

    jmp blink_led    ; Repeat the blinking cycle
delay:
    ; Simple delay loop
    mov cx, 1000     ; Set delay counter
delay_loop:
    dec cx
    jnz delay_loop   ; Loop until counter reaches
zero
    ret
```

In this example:

- We send commands ('1' and '0') to turn the LED on and off using the UART.
- A simple delay function (delay) is used to introduce a pause between turning the LED on and off, making it blink.

### Step 4: Running the Program

To run this program, you would need a development environment like **Microchip MPLAB X** or **Arduino IDE**, depending on your hardware. Once the program is uploaded to the microcontroller, the LED will blink continuously as the program sends alternating commands over UART.

---

## CONCLUSION

In this chapter, we've explored how low-level programs interface with external hardware using I/O ports and serial communication protocols such as UART, SPI, and I2C. We learned that I/O ports are critical communication channels between the CPU and hardware devices, and understanding the correct use of these ports is essential for efficient device interaction.

Through a hands-on example, we demonstrated how to write assembly code that interacts with external devices like an LED, using UART communication to control the LED's state. We also introduced basic serial protocols (UART, SPI, and I2C), which are the building blocks of communication in embedded systems.

Interfacing with external hardware is an essential skill in low-level systems programming, particularly in embedded systems and real-time applications. By mastering these techniques, you can develop applications that directly control devices, enabling precise and efficient hardware interactions.

# Chapter 11: Building a Custom Operating System (OS)

## 11.1 Introduction to Building a Custom OS at the Low Level

Building a custom operating system (OS) is one of the most challenging and rewarding tasks in systems programming. Unlike higher-level software development, where most of the hardware details are abstracted away, OS development requires you to directly manage system resources and interact with hardware.

At its core, an operating system is responsible for managing computer hardware, providing services for programs, and enabling communication between different software components. A custom OS is designed to control the hardware directly, handle system processes, and manage resources like memory, CPU, and I/O devices.

### 1. Why Build a Custom OS?

There are several reasons to build your own OS:

- **Learning Experience**: Building an OS from scratch helps you gain a deep understanding of how computers work at the lowest level. It gives you a direct connection to the hardware and teaches you about resource management, process scheduling, memory handling, and more.
- **Customizability**: Sometimes, pre-built OS solutions (like Linux or Windows) may not meet specific needs. A custom

OS allows you to tailor the system exactly to your requirements, whether it's for embedded systems, real-time systems, or educational purposes.
- **Performance and Efficiency**: A minimal OS can be highly optimized for specific tasks, offering better performance than general-purpose operating systems.

## 2. Key Components of an Operating System

An operating system typically consists of several key components:

- **Bootloader**: The small program that loads the OS kernel into memory when the system starts.
- **Kernel**: The core part of the OS that directly manages hardware resources, such as memory, processors, and input/output devices. It provides essential services like process scheduling, memory management, and system calls.
- **System Libraries**: These are collections of pre-written functions that provide basic services to programs, such as file handling or networking.
- **User Interface (UI)**: This is the interface through which users interact with the OS. It can be graphical (GUI) or command-line based (CLI).

---

## 11.2 BOOTSTRAPPING AND UNDERSTANDING THE BOOTLOADER PROCESS

Bootstrapping is the process of starting a computer from a powered-off state and loading the operating system. It involves several stages, starting with the BIOS (Basic Input/Output System) and leading to the execution of the operating system.

## 1. BIOS and the Bootstrap Process

When the computer is powered on, the **BIOS** or **UEFI** (Unified Extensible Firmware Interface) performs some initial hardware checks and configuration tasks. It then locates and loads a small piece of code called the **bootloader**, which is responsible for loading the actual operating system kernel into memory and starting its execution.

Here's a basic outline of the bootstrap process:

1. **Power-On**: The CPU receives power, and the BIOS/UEFI is executed.
2. **BIOS/UEFI**: Initializes hardware components like memory, CPU, and storage. The BIOS searches for a bootable device (like a hard drive or USB stick).
3. **Bootloader**: Once the BIOS finds the boot device, it loads the bootloader into memory and hands control over to it.
4. **Kernel Loading**: The bootloader loads the OS kernel from disk into memory and hands control over to the kernel.

## 2. Writing a Simple Bootloader

To build a custom OS, you first need to write a **bootloader**, which is responsible for loading your OS kernel. A bootloader is typically written in assembly language and is designed to work in a very constrained environment (limited memory and resources). It's the first piece of code that runs when the system starts.

Here's a minimal example of a simple bootloader:

```assembly
[bits 16]              ; 16-bit real mode
[org 0x7c00]           ; The bootloader is loaded
at 0x7c00
```

```
start:
    mov ah, 0x0e            ; BIOS teletype function
    mov al, 'H'             ; Load 'H' into AL
    int 0x10                ; Call BIOS interrupt to
print character
    mov al, 'i'
    int 0x10
    jmp $                   ; Infinite loop to stop
here

times 510 - ($ - $$) db 0  ; Fill the rest of the
bootloader with zeroes
dw 0xAA55                   ; Boot sector signature
(mandatory for booting)
```

This simple bootloader does the following:

1. **Prints "Hi" to the screen**: The `mov ah, 0x0e` and `int 0x10` instructions use BIOS interrupts to display characters on the screen.
2. **Infinite Loop**: The `jmp $` instruction creates an infinite loop, halting further execution, allowing the OS kernel to be loaded after this.

The bootloader's task is to display a message and hand over control to the kernel. The final line, `dw 0xAA55`, is the **boot sector signature**. It tells the BIOS that this is a valid bootable sector.

### 3. Loading the Kernel

Once the bootloader runs, its job is to load the operating system kernel into memory. The bootloader typically reads the kernel image from disk and copies it into memory. The kernel is then executed, and it takes control of the system.

For example, the bootloader might look for the kernel file (like `kernel.bin`), load it into memory, and jump to the kernel's entry point to start the OS.

## 11.3 BASIC KERNEL PROGRAMMING AND HOW TO MANAGE SYSTEM RESOURCES

Once the bootloader hands control over to the kernel, the kernel is responsible for managing system resources such as memory, CPU time, and I/O devices. Kernel programming requires direct interaction with hardware and low-level system components.

### 1. Managing Memory

In any operating system, memory management is one of the most critical tasks. The kernel must ensure that memory is allocated efficiently and that different processes don't interfere with each other's memory.

- **Memory Allocation**: The kernel manages both **static** memory (e.g., for the kernel code itself) and **dynamic** memory (e.g., for user programs).
- **Paging**: Most modern operating systems use a paging system for managing virtual memory. This allows programs to use more memory than is physically available by swapping data between RAM and disk storage.
- **Memory Protection**: The kernel prevents programs from accessing or modifying memory that they aren't authorized to use. This helps prevent crashes and ensures system stability.

## 2. Managing Processes

Process management refers to the creation, scheduling, and termination of processes. A **process** is a running instance of a program, and the kernel ensures that each process gets its fair share of CPU time.

- **Process Scheduling**: The kernel uses scheduling algorithms to determine which process gets CPU time next. This can be based on priority, time slices, or other factors.
- **Context Switching**: When switching between processes, the kernel saves the state of the current process (e.g., register values) and loads the state of the next process.

## 3. Managing I/O Devices

The kernel interacts with I/O devices through **device drivers**. These drivers are responsible for translating high-level OS requests into low-level hardware operations.

- **File System**: The kernel provides a file system that abstracts the underlying storage devices, allowing programs to read and write files without knowing how the data is physically stored.
- **Interrupts**: The kernel handles interrupts, which are signals from hardware devices indicating that they need attention. For example, a keyboard might generate an interrupt when a key is pressed.

## 11.4 HANDS-ON EXAMPLE: CREATING A MINIMAL BOOTABLE OS FROM SCRATCH

Now that we have covered the theory behind OS development, let's create a simple, bootable operating system. This minimal OS will demonstrate how to implement basic OS functionality such as loading from the bootloader and printing text to the screen.

### Step 1: Writing the Bootloader

The first step is to write a bootloader. As described earlier, this bootloader will display a simple message and load the kernel into memory. The bootloader is loaded by the BIOS at memory location 0x7C00, and once it runs, it will display "Hello, World!" on the screen.

```assembly
[bits 16]                    ; 16-bit real mode
[org 0x7c00]                 ; The bootloader is loaded
at 0x7c00

start:
    mov ah, 0x0e             ; BIOS teletype function
    mov al, 'H'              ; Load 'H' into AL
    int 0x10                 ; Call BIOS interrupt to
print character
    mov al, 'e'
    int 0x10
    mov al, 'l'
    int 0x10
    mov al, 'l'
    int 0x10
    mov al, 'o'
    int 0x10

    ; Jump to kernel (Assume the kernel is at 0x10000
in memory)
```

```
    jmp 0x1000:0x0000         ; Jump to the kernel's
entry point

times 510 - ($ - $$) db 0     ; Fill the rest of the
bootloader with zeroes
dw 0xAA55                     ; Boot sector signature
(mandatory for booting)
```

## Step 2: Writing the Kernel

Now let's write the kernel. The kernel will simply display "Kernel is running!" and then halt. This is the most basic form of a kernel.

assembly

```
[bits 16]                     ; 16-bit real mode
[org 0x1000]                  ; Kernel will load at
0x1000

start_kernel:
    mov ah, 0x0e              ; BIOS teletype function
    mov al, 'K'              ; Load 'K' into AL
    int 0x10                 ; Call BIOS interrupt to
print character
    mov al, 'e'
    int 0x10
    mov al, 'r'
    int 0x10
    mov al, 'n'
    int 0x10
    mov al, 'e'
    int 0x10
    mov al, 'l'
    int 0x10
    mov al, ' '
    int 0x10
    mov al, 'i'
    int 0x10
    mov al, 's'
    int 0x10
    mov al, ' '
    int 0x10
    mov al, 'r'
    int 0x10
```

```
mov al, 'u'
int 0x10
mov al, 'n'
int 0x10
mov al, 'n'
int 0x10
mov al, 'i'
int 0x10
mov al, 'n'
int 0x10
mov al, 'g'
int 0x10

; Halt the CPU (infinite loop)
jmp $
```

## Step 3: Creating the Bootable Disk Image

To create a bootable disk image that contains both the bootloader and the kernel, we need to:

1.  Compile the bootloader and kernel code into binary files.
2.  Create a bootable disk image that includes both files.

You can use tools like **NASM** (Netwide Assembler) to assemble the code and **dd** to create a bootable image.

1.  **Assemble the bootloader:**

    bash

    ```
    nasm -f bin bootloader.asm -o bootloader.bin
    ```

2.  **Assemble the kernel:**

    bash

    ```
    nasm -f bin kernel.asm -o kernel.bin
    ```

3.  **Create the bootable disk image:**

```bash
dd if=bootloader.bin of=boot.img bs=512 seek=1
dd if=kernel.bin of=boot.img bs=512 seek=4
```

4. **Run the OS in a virtual machine**: You can use tools like **QEMU** or **VirtualBox** to boot the OS and see the result.

```bash
qemu-system-x86_64 -drive
format=raw,file=boot.img
```

## CONCLUSION

In this chapter, we explored the fascinating world of building a custom operating system from scratch. We learned about the bootstrapping process and how to write a simple bootloader that loads the OS kernel into memory. We also wrote a basic kernel that prints text to the screen, showcasing the essentials of kernel programming.

Building an OS, even a minimal one, is a valuable experience for understanding how computer systems work at the most fundamental level. It forces you to learn about memory management, process scheduling, and hardware control, all of which are essential knowledge for anyone working in systems programming or embedded systems.

By following the steps outlined in this chapter, you've taken the first steps toward creating your own custom OS. From here, you can expand your OS by adding features such as memory management, multi-tasking, file systems, and device drivers.

# Chapter 12: Advanced Concepts in Low-Level Programming

## 12.1 WRITING EFFICIENT MULTI-THREADED ASSEMBLY PROGRAMS

Low-level programming allows you to interact with the hardware directly, giving you full control over how resources are managed and optimized. One of the most advanced and powerful concepts in modern systems programming is **multi-threading**—running multiple tasks simultaneously. While high-level languages offer built-in libraries for managing threads, in low-level programming (especially assembly), you need to manually handle the details of thread management.

### 1. The Basics of Multi-Threading

At the heart of multi-threading is the idea of executing different parts of a program simultaneously. Each thread represents an independent sequence of execution, and multi-threading allows for parallel processing of tasks. On modern multi-core processors, multi-threading can significantly improve performance by utilizing multiple cores to execute instructions concurrently.

- **Thread vs. Process**: A **process** is an independent program that runs in its own memory space, while a **thread** is a smaller unit of execution within a process that shares the same memory space. Multiple threads within a process can run in parallel, sharing resources and memory.

- **Thread Creation**: In assembly, creating threads involves setting up execution contexts for each thread. This typically includes defining memory regions for the stack and registers and setting up synchronization mechanisms to avoid conflicts when accessing shared resources.

## 2. Multi-Threading with Assembly

While multi-threading is common in high-level languages, it's less straightforward in assembly because there's no built-in thread management. Assembly programmers need to manually set up the environment for each thread, handle context switching, and synchronize threads.

In a low-level assembly program, managing threads involves:

- **Thread Stack**: Each thread must have its own stack to store local variables and execution context. The stack pointer must be managed for each thread separately.
- **Context Switching**: When the operating system switches between threads, it saves the state of the current thread (e.g., register values) and restores the state of the new thread. This process is called **context switching** and is essential for maintaining the illusion of parallel execution in multi-threaded programs.
- **Synchronization**: Since threads share memory, synchronizing access to shared resources is critical. Common methods include **mutexes** and **semaphores**, which control access to critical sections of code to prevent race conditions.

## 3. Implementing Multi-Threading in Assembly

To implement multi-threading in assembly, you would typically rely on the **operating system's scheduler** to handle context switching. Here's a basic example of how threads might be created and managed in a simple assembly program, using interrupts to simulate thread switching:

```assembly
section .data
    thread1 db "Thread 1 is running!", 0
    thread2 db "Thread 2 is running!", 0

section .text
    global _start

_start:
    ; Initialize first thread
    call thread1_function

    ; Initialize second thread
    call thread2_function

    ; Infinite loop to keep program running
    jmp $

thread1_function:
    ; Print message for thread 1
    mov edx, thread1
    call print_message
    ret

thread2_function:
    ; Print message for thread 2
    mov edx, thread2
    call print_message
    ret

print_message:
    ; Print the message pointed to by edx
    mov eax, 4
    mov ebx, 1
    int 0x80
    ret
```

This simple program simulates multi-threading by alternating between two functions that print messages. A real-world scenario would require synchronization, context switching, and managing the stack for each thread, but this example serves as a basic illustration.

### 4. Challenges of Multi-Threading in Assembly

While multi-threading can greatly improve performance, it also introduces significant complexity:

- **Race Conditions**: Multiple threads accessing shared data can lead to unpredictable results. Proper synchronization is crucial.
- **Stack Management**: Each thread needs its own stack to store local variables and function calls. Without proper management, the stacks can collide or overlap, causing errors.
- **Scheduling**: In assembly, managing which thread runs at any given time requires manually controlling the execution context. Most modern systems handle this with operating system schedulers, but writing a custom scheduler in assembly is complex.

## 12.2 IMPLEMENTING LOW-LEVEL NETWORKING PROTOCOLS (TCP/IP STACK IN ASSEMBLY)

Networking is an essential part of modern computing, and understanding how low-level networking protocols work is critical for building secure, efficient systems. **TCP/IP** (Transmission Control Protocol / Internet Protocol) is the foundation of the internet and is responsible for how data is transferred across networks.

## 1. Understanding TCP/IP and Network Layers

The **TCP/IP stack** is organized into four layers, each responsible for different aspects of communication:

- **Application Layer:** This is where network applications like web browsers, email clients, and file transfer programs operate. It uses protocols like HTTP and FTP.
- **Transport Layer:** This layer handles reliable data transfer between systems using protocols like TCP (connection-oriented) and UDP (connectionless).
- **Internet Layer:** Responsible for routing packets across networks, this layer uses the IP protocol to address and deliver data packets.
- **Link Layer:** Handles the physical transmission of data over network media, including Ethernet, Wi-Fi, and other hardware protocols.

## 2. Implementing Networking Protocols in Assembly

Writing a full TCP/IP stack from scratch in assembly is highly complex, but it's possible to implement simplified versions of key networking protocols. Here's an overview of how you might approach building a minimal network stack using assembly:

1. **Ethernet Frame:** The first step is understanding how to send and receive **Ethernet frames**. These frames contain the data needed to identify the sender, receiver, and protocol type. You would need to interact with the network card directly, sending raw Ethernet frames.
2. **IP Layer:** After understanding Ethernet, you can move on to the **Internet Protocol**. The IP header contains information such as the source and destination IP addresses, protocol type (e.g., TCP or UDP), and checksum for error checking.
3. **TCP/UDP Layer:** The next step involves implementing the transport layer. **TCP** is connection-oriented, meaning it

guarantees delivery and manages data flow control. **UDP**, on the other hand, is connectionless and faster, but it doesn't ensure delivery.

## 3. Writing Simple Networking Code in Assembly

Here's a simplified assembly example for sending a UDP packet (without a full TCP/IP stack) to demonstrate how low-level network communication might be handled. We'll assume that the hardware and driver are already configured, and the network interface is ready to send packets.

```assembly
; Simple UDP packet send (hypothetical, for
illustration only)

section .data
    destination_ip db 192, 168, 1, 1    ; IP address
of the destination
    source_port dw 12345                ; Source port
    dest_port dw 54321                  ; Destination
port
    message db 'Hello, Network!', 0

section .text
    global _start

_start:
    ; Prepare UDP header (simplified)
    ; Setup source and destination port, IP
addresses, etc.

    ; Send UDP packet
    ; (In a real program, this would involve
interacting with network hardware)
    mov eax, 0x01          ; Hypothetical system call
for sending data
    mov ebx, destination_ip  ; Load the destination
IP address
```

```
    mov ecx, dest_port      ; Load the destination
port
    mov edx, message        ; Load the message to send
    int 0x80                ; Call interrupt to send
the packet

    ; Exit the program
    mov eax, 1              ; System call number for
'exit'
    xor ebx, ebx           ; Exit status 0
    int 0x80               ; Invoke system call to
exit
```

This simple example demonstrates sending data over a network (although a real-world implementation would involve managing packet structures, checksums, and interfacing with the network hardware directly).

## 4. Challenges in Implementing Networking in Assembly

Writing networking code at such a low level is highly challenging because:

- **Hardware Abstraction**: Network interfaces are complex, and each hardware device has its own methods for sending and receiving data. Writing low-level network drivers and handling hardware interrupts is a significant challenge.
- **Protocol Complexity**: Protocols like TCP/IP involve many detailed steps, including checksums, packet fragmentation, retransmission strategies, and congestion control, all of which need to be implemented efficiently.
- **Error Handling**: Ensuring reliable communication, handling packet loss, and managing retries requires careful error handling and synchronization.

## 12.3 Understanding Low-Level Cryptography: How Encryption and Decryption Work at the Assembly Level

Cryptography is a critical aspect of security in modern systems. At its core, cryptography involves transforming data into a form that is unreadable to unauthorized parties and can only be decrypted by those with the correct key. Understanding how encryption and decryption work at the assembly level can give you insight into how secure systems are built.

### 1. Cryptographic Algorithms

There are two main types of cryptographic algorithms:

- **Symmetric Key Cryptography**: The same key is used for both encryption and decryption. Examples include **AES** and **DES**.
- **Asymmetric Key Cryptography**: Different keys are used for encryption and decryption. RSA is the most common example.

### 2. Basic Encryption at the Assembly Level

Implementing encryption algorithms at the assembly level can be complex because cryptographic algorithms usually involve multiple rounds of complex mathematical operations. Let's take **XOR** encryption as a simple example, where each byte of the message is XORed with a key byte.

**Example of XOR Encryption:**

```assembly
section .data
```

```asm
    key db 0xAA            ; Simple encryption key
    message db 'SecretMessage', 0

section .text
    global _start

_start:
    ; Loop through the message and XOR each byte with
the key
    mov si, message        ; Load the address of the
message
    mov al, [si]           ; Load the first byte of
the message

xor_loop:
    xor al, [key]          ; XOR the byte with the key
    mov [si], al           ; Store the encrypted byte
back
    inc si                 ; Move to the next byte
    cmp byte [si], 0       ; Check if we've reached
the end of the string
    je done
    mov al, [si]           ; Load the next byte
    jmp xor_loop

done:
    ; Exit the program
    mov eax, 1             ; System call number for
'exit'
    xor ebx, ebx           ; Exit status 0
    int 0x80               ; Invoke system call to
exit
```

In this simple example, the program uses XOR to encrypt a message. The xor instruction performs the bitwise XOR operation on the contents of the AL register with the key byte. This process is repeated for each byte of the message.

### 3. Decryption

The beauty of XOR encryption is that it's symmetric: the same operation is used for both encryption and decryption. To decrypt the message, you simply XOR the encrypted message again with the same key.

```assembly
; The same XOR encryption code can be used to decrypt
the message
```

### 4. Advanced Cryptographic Techniques

In real-world cryptographic algorithms like AES, multiple rounds of transformations are applied, and these involve complex bitwise operations, permutations, and substitutions. Implementing these algorithms in assembly is not trivial, but it can offer maximum performance.

For example, AES involves:

- **SubBytes**: A non-linear substitution step.
- **ShiftRows**: A permutation step.
- **MixColumns**: A diffusion step.
- **AddRoundKey**: An XOR operation with the round key.

### 5. Challenges in Implementing Cryptography in Assembly

- **Mathematical Complexity**: Modern encryption algorithms involve intricate mathematical operations that are difficult to implement manually in assembly.
- **Security Considerations**: Any small mistake in the implementation of cryptographic algorithms can create vulnerabilities. Cryptography is also vulnerable to side-channel attacks (e.g., timing attacks), which require careful implementation.

- **Performance**: While assembly can offer the best performance, encryption algorithms like AES need to handle large amounts of data efficiently, which can be difficult in low-level programming.

---

## 12.4 HANDS-ON EXAMPLE: WRITING AN ASSEMBLY PROGRAM THAT ENCRYPTS AND DECRYPTS MESSAGES

Let's implement a basic example of **Caesar cipher encryption** in assembly. The Caesar cipher is a simple encryption technique where each letter in the plaintext is shifted by a certain number of positions in the alphabet.

### Step 1: Implementing Caesar Cipher Encryption

assembly

```
section .data
    message db 'HELLO', 0  ; Plaintext message
    shift db 3             ; Shift key (e.g., shift
by 3)

section .text
    global _start

_start:
    mov si, message        ; Point to the message
    mov bl, [shift]        ; Load the shift value

encrypt_loop:
    mov al, [si]           ; Load the current
character
    cmp al, 0              ; Check if it's the null
terminator
    je done                ; If it is, finish
```

```
    sub al, 'A'              ; Convert letter to 0-25
range
    add al, bl               ; Shift the letter
    mod 26                   ; Wrap around using modulo
26
    add al, 'A'              ; Convert back to ASCII
    mov [si], al             ; Store the encrypted
character
    inc si                   ; Move to the next
character
    jmp encrypt_loop

done:
    ; Exit program
    mov eax, 1               ; System call number for
'exit'
    xor ebx, ebx             ; Exit status 0
    int 0x80                 ; Invoke system call to
exit
```

## Step 2: Decrypting the Message

The decryption process is simply the inverse of encryption. To decrypt, we shift the letters backward by the same key.

```
assembly
```

```
; Decrypt using the reverse shift
```

This example demonstrates how simple encryption and decryption can be done in assembly.

---

## CONCLUSION

In this chapter, we've explored several advanced concepts in low-level programming, including multi-threading, networking, and cryptography. We covered how to write efficient multi-threaded programs in assembly, implement low-level networking protocols like TCP/IP, and understand how encryption and decryption work at the assembly level.

Through hands-on examples, we demonstrated how to encrypt and decrypt messages using simple encryption techniques like XOR and Caesar cipher. We also examined the challenges involved in implementing more complex cryptographic algorithms and managing multi-threading and networking at the assembly level.

These advanced topics are essential for anyone looking to master low-level systems programming. By understanding the underlying principles of multi-threading, networking, and cryptography, you'll be able to build more efficient, secure, and optimized systems.

# Chapter 13: Building Real-World Applications in Low-Level Systems Programming

## 13.1 How to Use Assembly and Machine Language in Real-World Applications such as Robotics, Embedded Systems, and IoT

Low-level programming, particularly through assembly and machine language, is integral to creating applications that require direct interaction with hardware. While high-level languages abstract away much of the complexity, low-level programming allows for finely tuned performance and control, which is crucial in areas like robotics, embedded systems, and the Internet of Things (IoT).

### 1. The Role of Assembly in Embedded Systems

An **embedded system** is a specialized computer designed to perform a specific task. Embedded systems are found in countless devices, such as cars, microwaves, industrial machines, and medical devices. The reason low-level programming is often used in embedded systems is due to the need for efficiency, real-time performance, and resource-constrained environments.

- **Direct Hardware Control**: Low-level languages, especially assembly, allow direct manipulation of hardware registers, memory, and I/O ports. This level of control is crucial for optimizing performance in embedded devices.

- **Minimal Resource Use**: Embedded systems often operate on limited resources (CPU, memory, and storage). Using assembly or machine language ensures that the program uses as little memory and processing power as possible.
- **Real-Time Constraints**: Many embedded systems are required to meet real-time performance constraints. Low-level programming allows developers to ensure that code executes with minimal delay, meeting the timing requirements.

## 2. Assembly in Robotics

Robotics is another area where low-level programming plays a pivotal role. Robots often require direct control over motors, sensors, and other hardware components, making it necessary to interact with the underlying hardware in an efficient manner.

- **Sensor Integration**: Low-level programming allows for precise reading and control of sensor data. Sensors such as ultrasonic sensors, accelerometers, and gyroscopes often provide raw data that needs to be processed and interpreted in real-time.
- **Motor Control**: Robotics involves controlling motors and actuators. Using assembly or machine language allows for fine-grained control of motors, ensuring precise movement and reducing latency.
- **Performance Optimization**: Real-time response is crucial in robotics. By using assembly, robotics systems can minimize delays in data processing, motion control, and feedback loops.

## 3. Assembly in Internet of Things (IoT)

The **Internet of Things (IoT)** refers to a network of physical devices embedded with sensors, software, and other technologies to collect and exchange data. Many IoT devices are constrained by power, memory, and processing capacity, which makes assembly and machine language highly suitable for these applications.

- **Power Efficiency**: IoT devices often run on battery power. Low-level programming helps to optimize energy consumption, making it possible for devices to run longer on limited resources.
- **Optimized Communication**: IoT devices need to communicate efficiently over networks, whether through Wi-Fi, Bluetooth, or Zigbee. Assembly allows for minimizing the overhead involved in data transmission, making communication faster and more reliable.
- **Sensor Data Processing**: IoT devices commonly collect data from various sensors (temperature, humidity, motion, etc.). Assembly is used to handle the sensor data processing efficiently, enabling real-time analysis and immediate action based on input.

## 13.2 OVERVIEW OF THE HARDWARE-SOFTWARE INTERACTION IN INDUSTRIES LIKE HEALTHCARE, LOGISTICS, AND MANUFACTURING

Low-level systems programming is indispensable in various industries, where it directly influences performance, safety, and efficiency. In fields like healthcare, logistics, and manufacturing, real-time control and optimal resource utilization are paramount. Let's examine how hardware and software interact in these industries, with a focus on low-level programming.

# 1. Healthcare: Embedded Systems and Real-Time Monitoring

The healthcare industry heavily relies on embedded systems for critical applications such as medical devices, patient monitoring, and diagnostic equipment. These systems often require precise control over sensors, actuators, and communication devices, which can be achieved through low-level programming.

- **Medical Devices**: Devices like pacemakers, infusion pumps, and EEG monitors require direct access to hardware to monitor patient vitals, adjust settings, and ensure safety. Assembly programming is used to write firmware that ensures the precise operation of these devices.
- **Real-Time Data Processing**: Many medical applications, such as heart rate monitors and blood glucose meters, require real-time data processing. Low-level systems programming ensures that these devices operate without delays, providing accurate and timely data.
- **Data Acquisition**: Sensors like thermometers, blood pressure cuffs, and glucose meters require direct interfacing with microcontrollers. Assembly allows for reading raw sensor data, processing it, and sending it to a display or storage system.

# 2. Logistics: Real-Time Systems for Tracking and Control

Logistics involves the management of goods and services as they move through supply chains. Real-time systems are crucial in logistics for tracking shipments, managing inventories, and ensuring timely delivery. Low-level programming helps optimize the performance of embedded systems used in logistics.

- **Tracking Devices**: Modern logistics systems use RFID tags, GPS, and other sensors to track the location and status of goods. Low-level programming is used to interface with these sensors, process the data, and transmit it to central systems.

- **Warehouse Automation**: Automated guided vehicles (AGVs) and robotic arms are used to move items in warehouses. Low-level programming ensures these systems respond in real-time, allowing for efficient and safe operations.
- **Network Communication**: Real-time communication between sensors, databases, and central control systems is essential. Low-level network protocols (e.g., TCP/IP or UDP) are used to send and receive data quickly, ensuring minimal latency in communication.

## 3. Manufacturing: Embedded Systems for Control and Automation

In manufacturing, embedded systems are used to control machinery, manage production lines, and optimize workflows. Real-time control of machines and automation systems is critical to ensuring high efficiency and safety.

- **Machine Control**: CNC machines, robotic arms, and 3D printers all require precise control over motors, sensors, and actuators. Low-level programming ensures the hardware responds accurately to control signals, enabling high-quality production.
- **Automation Systems**: Modern manufacturing plants use automation systems to monitor and control production processes. Low-level programming is used to interface with PLCs (Programmable Logic Controllers), sensors, and actuators, ensuring smooth operations with minimal downtime.
- **Quality Control**: Sensors that measure temperature, pressure, and product dimensions are used for quality assurance. Low-level systems programming handles the integration of these sensors and processes the data in real-time, ensuring product quality standards are met.

# 13.3 Hands-On Example: Building a Simple Embedded System (e.g., a Temperature Sensor)

In this section, we will create a simple embedded system that reads data from a temperature sensor and displays the value on a screen. The system will use low-level programming to directly interact with the hardware.

## 1. Overview of the System

We will use the following components:

- **Microcontroller**: This will be the heart of our embedded system, controlling the temperature sensor and managing the data.
- **Temperature Sensor (e.g., LM35)**: This sensor will measure temperature and output an analog signal.
- **Display**: We'll use a simple 7-segment display or an LED array to show the temperature.
- **Power Supply**: The system will run on a small power supply, such as a battery or USB power.

## 2. Setting Up the Microcontroller

Let's assume we are using a basic 8-bit microcontroller (like the **8051** or **AVR** series). We need to configure the microcontroller's I/O ports to read the sensor data and send it to the display.

First, initialize the necessary I/O pins:

```
assembly

; Initialize microcontroller ports
mov P1, #0xFF        ; Set Port 1 to input mode (sensor
connected here)
mov P2, #0x00        ; Set Port 2 to output mode
(display connected here)
```

### 3. Interfacing with the Temperature Sensor

Assume that the LM35 sensor outputs a voltage proportional to the temperature in Celsius (10mV per degree Celsius). We will use an **Analog-to-Digital Converter (ADC)** to convert the analog voltage into a digital value that the microcontroller can process.

```
assembly

; Read analog value from LM35 (using an ADC)
mov A, ADC_DATA      ; Get ADC data
```

In real-world systems, you would use a separate ADC module to convert the sensor's analog output to a digital value. Here, ADC_DATA would contain the 8-bit digital representation of the temperature value.

### 4. Converting Sensor Data to Temperature

After reading the ADC value, we need to convert it into a temperature value. Since each increment in the ADC value represents a fixed amount of temperature change (based on the sensor's characteristics), we can map the ADC value to a temperature range.

For simplicity, let's assume the ADC value corresponds directly to the temperature in degrees Celsius. In a more advanced system, you would scale the value based on the sensor's calibration.

```assembly
; Assume A contains the ADC value (0-255 range)
mov B, A              ; Copy ADC value to B for
processing
```

## 5. Displaying the Temperature

Next, we'll send the temperature value to the display. For simplicity, let's assume a basic 7-segment display that takes a single byte (0-255 range) and converts it to the corresponding digit.

```assembly
; Send temperature value to the display
mov P2, B             ; Output the temperature value to
Port 2 (display)
```

In this case, P2 is the port connected to the 7-segment display, and the value in B corresponds to the temperature to be displayed.

## 6. Adding Delay and Looping

To keep the system running continuously and update the display at regular intervals, we need to add a delay and loop the program.

```assembly
; Delay function
delay:
    mov R0, #255       ; Load delay value
delay_loop:
    nop                ; No operation (do nothing for
1 clock cycle)
    nop
    nop
    dec R0
    jnz delay_loop
    ret

; Main program loop
```

```
main_loop:
    call delay              ; Wait before reading sensor
again
    jmp main_loop           ; Loop indefinitely
```

This program will continuously read the temperature sensor, convert the data, and display it on the screen.

---

## 13.4 CHALLENGES IN LOW-LEVEL PROGRAMMING FOR REAL-WORLD APPLICATIONS

Building real-world applications in low-level systems programming is an incredibly rewarding but challenging task. The challenges include:

- **Resource Constraints**: Embedded systems often run on very limited resources (memory, processing power, etc.), making efficient programming critical.
- **Real-Time Requirements**: Many applications, such as robotics or healthcare devices, require real-time performance. Achieving low latency and predictable behavior is crucial.
- **Hardware Variability**: Different hardware platforms require specific knowledge about their architecture, I/O interfaces, and peripherals. This requires custom-tailored programming for each device.
- **Debugging**: Debugging low-level programs can be difficult due to the lack of high-level abstractions. Tools like oscilloscopes, logic analyzers, and debuggers become essential in diagnosing issues.
- **Power Efficiency**: Many embedded devices run on battery power, so optimizing code for minimal power consumption is a key factor in system design.

## CONCLUSION

In this chapter, we've explored how low-level programming is used in real-world applications like robotics, embedded systems, and the Internet of Things (IoT). We delved into how assembly and machine language allow for efficient, resource-constrained systems that interact directly with hardware.

We also examined how these concepts apply in industries like healthcare, logistics, and manufacturing, where performance, real-time response, and system reliability are paramount. By building a simple embedded system to interface with a temperature sensor, we demonstrated how low-level systems programming can be used to create real-world, hardware-driven applications.

While building embedded systems and IoT applications using assembly poses unique challenges, it offers unmatched control and performance. The knowledge gained from creating these systems lays a solid foundation for tackling even more complex projects in the future.

# Chapter 14: The Future of Low-Level Programming

## 14.1 EMERGING TRENDS IN LOW-LEVEL SYSTEMS PROGRAMMING

Low-level programming has been a cornerstone of computing for decades, allowing developers to communicate directly with hardware and build the most efficient, performance-oriented applications. While high-level programming languages have gained popularity for their ease of use, low-level programming still plays a crucial role in many modern technologies. Emerging trends in computing, such as quantum computing, AI, and machine learning, are bringing new challenges and opportunities for low-level systems programming.

### 1. Automation and AI-Assisted Programming

One of the most exciting trends in low-level systems programming is the advent of AI-assisted programming tools. While low-level programming typically requires deep expertise, AI and machine learning can help automate aspects of the development process.

- **Code Generation**: AI tools can generate boilerplate code or assist with repetitive tasks, allowing developers to focus on more complex parts of the system. For example, AI can be used to suggest optimized assembly code based on high-level specifications, helping developers write code that is more efficient and error-free.

- **Bug Detection:** Machine learning can be trained to identify common errors and vulnerabilities in low-level code, such as memory leaks, race conditions, and buffer overflows. These AI systems can also suggest optimizations for performance bottlenecks in assembly code.
- **Automated Optimization:** AI algorithms are being developed to automatically optimize low-level code. These tools can analyze the structure of assembly or machine language code and suggest or apply changes that improve execution time, memory usage, or power consumption.

## 2. Cross-Platform Development and Compilation

As computing devices become increasingly diverse, from traditional desktops to embedded systems, mobile devices, and edge computing devices, there's a growing demand for cross-platform compatibility in low-level programming.

- **Cross-Platform Compilers:** Compilers that can generate assembly code for different architectures are becoming more advanced. Tools that support cross-compilation for different microcontrollers, GPUs, and processors enable developers to write low-level code that can run across various platforms without significant changes.
- **Virtualization:** Virtual machines (VMs) and containerization technologies like Docker are making it easier to develop and test low-level code in isolated environments. These tools allow developers to create portable and reproducible low-level development environments that can run on different hardware configurations.

## 3. Low-Level Programming for Edge and IoT Devices

With the explosion of the Internet of Things (IoT) and edge computing, there is an increasing need for low-level programming that can run on highly constrained devices. These devices often have limited memory, processing power, and energy resources, making low-level programming essential for optimizing performance.

- **Energy Efficiency**: Low-level programming is critical for ensuring that devices can operate efficiently on limited power sources, such as batteries or energy harvested from the environment. Developers must carefully manage power consumption, particularly in wireless sensor networks and wearables.
- **Real-Time Processing**: Many IoT applications require real-time data processing, such as environmental monitoring, industrial automation, and autonomous vehicles. Low-level programming is necessary for meeting strict timing and latency requirements in these systems.
- **Security**: IoT devices are frequently targeted by cyber-attacks due to their reliance on software with limited resources. Low-level programming allows for the development of secure, lightweight software that ensures the integrity of communications and data.

## 4. The Role of Low-Level Programming in Modern Hardware Architectures

Emerging hardware architectures, such as GPUs, FPGAs, and specialized processors like Tensor Processing Units (TPUs) for machine learning, are driving the need for more efficient low-level programming. Low-level programming is key to unlocking the full potential of these new architectures.

- **GPUs**: Graphics Processing Units are widely used for parallel computing tasks, including machine learning, simulation, and gaming. Low-level programming in CUDA or OpenCL allows developers to leverage the massive parallelism of GPUs for high-performance applications.
- **FPGAs**: Field-Programmable Gate Arrays are customizable hardware devices that can be programmed to perform

specific tasks very efficiently. Low-level programming is essential for configuring FPGAs to handle specialized tasks, such as signal processing, cryptography, or custom accelerators for deep learning.

- **TPUs:** As machine learning grows, hardware accelerators like TPUs are gaining popularity. These processors are optimized for high-throughput operations on matrices and tensors, commonly used in deep learning. Low-level programming is necessary to fine-tune the hardware to perform these operations efficiently.

## 14.2 THE ROLE OF LOW-LEVEL PROGRAMMING IN MODERN TECHNOLOGIES SUCH AS AI, MACHINE LEARNING, AND QUANTUM COMPUTING

Low-level programming is becoming increasingly intertwined with cutting-edge technologies like AI, machine learning, and quantum computing. While these technologies often rely on high-level programming languages and frameworks, the underlying systems that power these applications are often built using low-level code to optimize performance and efficiency.

### 1. Low-Level Programming in Artificial Intelligence (AI)

Artificial intelligence, particularly in areas like deep learning and neural networks, benefits significantly from low-level programming.

- **Optimization:** Machine learning frameworks like TensorFlow and PyTorch rely on low-level libraries and assembly code to perform matrix multiplications and other computationally expensive operations. Customizing low-level code for specific hardware can lead to massive performance improvements, especially when running AI models on GPUs or specialized hardware.

- **Custom Hardware Accelerators**: Low-level programming is often used to develop custom hardware accelerators for AI workloads. For instance, custom-built ASICs (Application-Specific Integrated Circuits) or FPGAs can be optimized to perform specific AI operations faster and with lower power consumption.
- **Real-Time AI Systems**: Low-level programming is crucial for real-time AI systems, where latency is a critical factor. For example, AI systems for autonomous driving or industrial robots require near-instantaneous decision-making. Low-level programming ensures that these systems can process sensor data and make decisions quickly and accurately.

## 2. Low-Level Programming in Machine Learning

Machine learning relies on large-scale computations, often involving huge datasets and complex algorithms. Low-level programming can be used to optimize the implementation of machine learning algorithms, particularly for training and inference tasks.

- **Neural Network Training**: Training deep neural networks involves processing large amounts of data and performing many floating-point operations. Writing low-level code that takes advantage of hardware accelerators (like GPUs or TPUs) can significantly speed up training times.
- **Inference Optimization**: Once a model is trained, it must be deployed to make predictions in real-time. Low-level programming is used to optimize the inference process, ensuring that models can be executed on devices with limited resources, such as smartphones or embedded systems.

## 3. Low-Level Programming in Quantum Computing

Quantum computing is a revolutionary field that promises to solve problems that are intractable for classical computers. While quantum programming languages like Qiskit and Cirq abstract away many details, low-level programming still plays a vital role in quantum computing.

- **Quantum Hardware Interaction**: Quantum computers rely on specialized hardware, such as superconducting qubits or trapped ions. Low-level programming is necessary to interact with this hardware, ensuring that quantum algorithms are correctly translated into operations that manipulate qubits.
- **Quantum Assembly**: Quantum programming languages often compile down to lower-level instructions that interact directly with quantum processors. Just like classical assembly, quantum assembly is used to control qubit operations like gates, measurements, and entanglements.
- **Quantum Simulation**: Simulating quantum systems on classical computers is another area where low-level programming plays a crucial role. Simulations of quantum systems require significant computational power, and low-level optimizations can help improve the efficiency of these simulations.

## 14.3 ASSEMBLY LANGUAGE IN THE CONTEXT OF QUANTUM COMPUTERS AND OTHER NEXT-GENERATION TECHNOLOGIES

While quantum computing is still in its infancy, it holds immense promise for fields like cryptography, optimization, and machine learning. As quantum computing hardware evolves, so will the need for low-level programming techniques to ensure efficient execution of quantum algorithms.

## 1. Quantum Assembly Language

Quantum assembly language, or **QASM** (Quantum Assembly Language), is a low-level language that enables developers to directly interact with quantum computers. It serves as the intermediate step between high-level quantum algorithms and the operations that control qubits. Writing quantum programs in assembly gives developers the flexibility to control the precise operations of quantum gates, measurements, and entanglements.

Quantum assembly programs are written in a manner similar to classical assembly. For example, a quantum gate (analogous to classical logical operations) might look like this in quantum assembly:

```qasm
// Apply Hadamard gate to qubit 0
h q[0];

// Apply CNOT gate between qubits 0 and 1
cx q[0], q[1];
```

## 2. Hybrid Systems: Classical and Quantum Integration

While quantum computers are still being developed, **hybrid systems**—which integrate classical and quantum computing—are becoming increasingly important. In these systems, classical computers handle tasks that are well-suited for traditional computing (such as managing data and performing basic computations), while quantum computers handle tasks that require quantum algorithms (such as simulating molecular structures or solving complex optimization problems).

Low-level programming plays a critical role in ensuring smooth communication between classical and quantum components. For example, assembly or machine language could be used to efficiently manage data exchanges between classical processors and quantum processors.

### 3. Other Next-Generation Technologies

Beyond quantum computing, other next-generation technologies—such as neuromorphic computing, brain-computer interfaces (BCI), and edge AI—are beginning to emerge. These technologies often rely on low-level programming to ensure that they run efficiently on specialized hardware.

- **Neuromorphic Computing**: This field involves building hardware systems that mimic the structure and function of the human brain. Low-level programming is used to control the hardware and optimize its performance.
- **Brain-Computer Interfaces (BCI)**: BCIs enable direct communication between the brain and external devices. Low-level programming is crucial for real-time data processing, signal amplification, and communication between the brain and external hardware.
- **Edge AI**: As AI moves to the edge, where computations occur closer to the data source, low-level programming ensures that AI models can be efficiently deployed on resource-constrained devices such as smartphones, drones, and wearables.

# 14.4 Hands-On Example: Exploring Low-Level Programming on New Hardware Platforms (e.g., Quantum Computing Simulators)

To conclude this chapter, let's explore a hands-on example using a quantum computing simulator. While writing low-level programs for quantum hardware may not yet be practical for most people, quantum simulators offer an excellent way to experiment with quantum algorithms and assembly code.

## 1. Setting Up the Quantum Simulator

For this example, we'll use the **Qiskit** library, which is a quantum computing framework developed by IBM. Qiskit allows developers to write quantum programs, simulate them, and run them on real quantum hardware.

1. **Install Qiskit**: First, install Qiskit via pip:

   bash

   ```
   pip install qiskit
   ```

2. **Create a Quantum Circuit**: We'll create a simple quantum circuit that uses a **Hadamard gate** (which creates superposition) and a **CNOT gate** (which entangles two qubits).

   python

   ```
   from qiskit import QuantumCircuit, Aer, execute

   # Create a quantum circuit with 2 qubits
   qc = QuantumCircuit(2)

   # Apply a Hadamard gate to qubit 0
   qc.h(0)
   ```

```python
# Apply a CNOT gate to qubits 0 and 1
qc.cx(0, 1)

# Visualize the quantum circuit
print(qc)
```

3. **Simulate the Quantum Circuit**: We'll use Qiskit's **Aer simulator** to simulate the quantum circuit. The Aer simulator runs on classical computers but mimics the behavior of quantum hardware.

```python
python

simulator =
Aer.get_backend('statevector_simulator')

# Execute the circuit on the simulator
result = execute(qc, simulator).result()

# Print the result (state vector)
print(result.get_statevector())
```

## 2. Interpreting the Results

The output from the simulator represents the state vector of the quantum system, which contains information about the probability amplitudes of different quantum states. By measuring the qubits, we can collapse the superposition and get classical results.

```python
python

# Measure the qubits and print the result
qc.measure_all()

# Execute the circuit with measurements
result = execute(qc, simulator, shots=1024).result()

# Print the counts (frequency of measurement
outcomes)
print(result.get_counts())
```

This example simulates a quantum algorithm in a quantum computing simulator. While the program runs on classical hardware, it provides insights into how low-level programming in quantum systems works.

---

## CONCLUSION

In this chapter, we explored the future of low-level systems programming, examining the emerging trends in multi-threading, cross-platform development, and hardware-software interaction. We looked at how low-level programming is becoming increasingly important in modern technologies such as AI, machine learning, quantum computing, and other next-generation hardware.

We also explored the role of low-level programming in AI and quantum computing, and how it is used to optimize performance in specialized hardware like GPUs, FPGAs, and quantum processors. Through a hands-on example, we demonstrated how to create quantum circuits and use quantum simulators for low-level programming in quantum computing.

As we move into the future, low-level programming will continue to play a critical role in shaping the next generation of technologies. By mastering low-level systems programming, developers can create highly optimized software that takes full advantage of emerging hardware and computational paradigms.

# Chapter 15: Final Project: Building a High-Performance Low-Level Application

## 15.1 PUTTING IT ALL TOGETHER: DESIGN AND DEVELOP A COMPLEX LOW-LEVEL APPLICATION

In the world of low-level programming, creating a complex application from scratch is both an exciting and challenging endeavor. Low-level programming requires a deep understanding of how software interacts with hardware and the ability to optimize resources at the most fundamental levels. Whether you are working on a **real-time operating system (RTOS)**, developing a **network driver**, or building a specialized **embedded system**, the principles of design, coding, testing, and optimization remain critical to ensuring the application's success.

In this chapter, we will walk through the process of designing, coding, and optimizing a **high-performance low-level application** from the ground up. Specifically, we will develop a **custom network protocol stack** using **assembly language**, focusing on efficiency, reliability, and real-time performance.

1. The Importance of Low-Level Application Design

Low-level application development involves several key considerations:

- **Performance Optimization**: Low-level code runs directly on the hardware, so efficient resource management—especially CPU time, memory, and I/O—is critical. Poorly written low-level code can lead to significant performance bottlenecks, which is why careful optimization is a key part of the process.
- **Resource Constraints**: In many low-level systems, resources such as memory and processing power are often limited. This is especially true for embedded systems and IoT devices. Low-level programming must take into account these limitations and ensure that the application can function within these constraints.
- **Real-Time Constraints**: Low-level applications often need to meet stringent real-time performance requirements, especially in systems like operating systems, network drivers, and robotics. Ensuring that the system can process events and handle interrupts in a timely manner is essential.
- **Reliability and Error Handling**: Low-level applications, especially those interacting with hardware, must handle errors gracefully. Implementing robust error-handling routines is crucial, particularly in critical systems such as network drivers or medical devices.

## 2. Setting the Scope of the Project

Before starting the development of any low-level application, it's important to define the scope of the project. This involves identifying the core functionality, performance requirements, hardware limitations, and real-time constraints.

For our project, we will create a **custom network protocol stack** from scratch using assembly language. The stack will handle low-level communication between devices over a network, implementing protocols like **Ethernet, IP, TCP**, and **UDP**. We'll focus on writing the protocols from the ground up, simulating packet handling, and managing the interactions between different layers of the stack.

## 15.2 STEP-BY-STEP GUIDE TO PLANNING, CODING, TESTING, AND OPTIMIZING THE APPLICATION

### 1. Planning the Application

The first step in any low-level application development process is to plan the structure and behavior of the system. This phase involves determining the key components, their interactions, and the overall architecture of the application.

For our custom network protocol stack, we will break it down into the following layers:

1. **Ethernet Layer**: Handles the low-level frame structure, including MAC addresses and frame check sequences (FCS).
2. **IP Layer**: Implements the Internet Protocol (IPv4), which handles packet routing, addressing, and fragmentation.
3. **Transport Layer**: Implements TCP (Transmission Control Protocol) and UDP (User Datagram Protocol), responsible for managing connections, data streams, and error handling.
4. **Application Layer**: While our focus will be on the lower layers, an application layer can be added to simulate higher-level protocols like HTTP or FTP.

Each layer will interact with the underlying hardware or simulate communication using predefined interfaces. The stack will need to handle the following:

- **Packet creation** and **parsing**.
- **Checksums** and **error detection**.

- **Connection management** (in the case of TCP).
- **Sending and receiving packets** through the network interface card (NIC).

## 2. Coding the Application

Now that we have our architecture, the next step is to begin coding each layer of the protocol stack. We'll start by creating the **Ethernet layer** in assembly language.

### Ethernet Layer

Ethernet frames consist of the following fields:

- **Preamble:** Synchronization field.
- **Destination MAC Address:** 6 bytes.
- **Source MAC Address:** 6 bytes.
- **EtherType:** 2 bytes, indicating the type of protocol being encapsulated (e.g., IP).
- **Payload:** Data.
- **Frame Check Sequence (FCS):** 4 bytes used for error detection.

Here is a simple example of creating an Ethernet frame in assembly:

```assembly
assembly

section .data
    dest_mac db 0x00, 0x1A, 0x2B, 0x3C, 0x4D, 0x5E
; Destination MAC address
    src_mac db 0x00, 0x1A, 0x2B, 0x3C, 0x4D, 0x6F
; Source MAC address
    ethertype dw 0x0800
; EtherType for IPv4
    payload db 'Hello, Network!', 0x00
; Payload (data)

section .bss
```

```
    eth_frame resb 64    ; Reserve space for the
Ethernet frame

section .text
    global _start

_start:
    ; Construct Ethernet frame
    mov esi, eth_frame     ; Load the frame buffer
address

    ; Copy destination MAC address
    mov edi, dest_mac
    movsb                  ; Move source byte to
destination

    ; Copy source MAC address
    mov edi, src_mac
    movsb                  ; Move source byte to
destination

    ; Copy EtherType
    mov ax, ethertype
    mov [esi], ax
    add esi, 2             ; Move to the next
position in frame

    ; Copy payload
    mov edi, payload
    movsb                  ; Move source byte to
destination

    ; End of frame construction
    ; (Next steps would involve adding the FCS and
sending the frame over the network)
```

This code constructs an Ethernet frame by copying the source and
destination MAC addresses, EtherType, and payload into a buffer.

## IP Layer

The IP layer handles packet routing, addressing, and fragmentation. We'll implement a basic IPv4 header, which includes:

- **Version and IHL** (Internet Header Length).
- **Type of Service**.
- **Total Length**.
- **Identification, Flags,** and **Fragment Offset**.
- **Time to Live (TTL)**.
- **Protocol** (TCP/UDP).
- **Source and Destination IP Addresses.**

Here's how we might begin constructing an IPv4 header:

```assembly
section .data
    src_ip db 192, 168, 1, 1  ; Source IP address
    dest_ip db 192, 168, 1, 2 ; Destination IP
address

section .bss
    ip_packet resb 20         ; Reserve space for the
IP header

section .text
    global _start

_start:
    ; Create IPv4 header
    mov esi, ip_packet        ; Load IP header buffer
address

    ; Version and IHL
    mov al, 0x45              ; IPv4, header length =
5 words
    mov [esi], al
    add esi, 1                ; Move to next field
```

```
    ; Type of Service
    mov byte [esi], 0x00
    add esi, 1                  ; Move to next field

    ; Total Length
    mov word [esi], 0x00        ; Placeholder for total
length
    add esi, 2                  ; Move to next field

    ; Next fields (Identification, TTL, Protocol,
Source/Dest IP) would follow similarly
```

We'll need to handle checksums, routing, and fragmenting the packet as part of the full implementation. The IP layer will also be responsible for interfacing with the hardware to send packets.

## Transport Layer (TCP/UDP)

The transport layer is where the real complexity begins. For simplicity, let's assume we are implementing **UDP** (User Datagram Protocol), which is connectionless and doesn't involve the complexities of connection management that TCP does.

A UDP packet consists of the following fields:

- **Source Port**.
- **Destination Port**.
- **Length**.
- **Checksum**.

Here's a simple outline of the UDP header construction:

assembly

```
section .data
    src_port dw 12345           ; Source port
    dest_port dw 54321          ; Destination port
    udp_length dw 8             ; Length of UDP header
```

```asm
section .bss
    udp_packet resb 8          ; Reserve space for
the UDP header

section .text
    global _start

_start:
    ; Construct UDP header
    mov esi, udp_packet        ; Load UDP packet
buffer address

    ; Source Port
    mov ax, [src_port]         ; Load source port into
ax
    mov [esi], ax              ; Store source port
    add esi, 2                 ; Move to next field

    ; Destination Port
    mov ax, [dest_port]        ; Load destination port
    mov [esi], ax              ; Store destination
port
    add esi, 2                 ; Move to next field

    ; Length
    mov ax, [udp_length]       ; Load UDP packet
length
    mov [esi], ax              ; Store length
    add esi, 2                 ; Move to next field

    ; Checksum would be calculated and added
```

In a full implementation, you would also compute the **checksum** for the UDP header and data. UDP provides minimal error checking, unlike TCP.

## 3. Testing the Application

Testing a custom network protocol stack involves simulating communication between devices. We can test the various layers by simulating data packets and observing whether the stack correctly processes and forwards them.

To test the Ethernet layer, for example, you could send a custom Ethernet frame from one device to another, verifying that the destination MAC address is correct. Similarly, the IP layer can be tested by sending packets with specific source and destination IP addresses.

## 4. Optimizing the Application

Once the basic stack is built, performance optimization becomes a priority. Some areas to focus on include:

- **Minimizing Memory Usage**: Low-level applications often run on memory-constrained systems, so optimizing memory usage is crucial. Consider using memory pools, buffers, and static allocation rather than dynamic memory allocation.
- **Latency Reduction**: In networking applications, minimizing latency is essential. Low-level optimizations like reducing interrupt handling time, using direct memory access (DMA) for I/O, and efficient memory access patterns can improve performance.
- **Parallelism and Multithreading**: Modern systems often have multiple cores. Using low-level threading mechanisms and optimizing synchronization can help achieve parallelism and improve throughput.

## 15.3 Hands-On Example: Building a Custom Network Protocol Stack from Scratch Using Assembly Language

Let's break down a simple example of building a **custom network protocol stack** from scratch. This stack will simulate basic Ethernet, IP, and UDP functionality, allowing for simple packet transmission and routing.

### Step 1: Setting Up the Environment

We'll need an environment to test and simulate the network stack:

1. **Operating System**: Use a custom OS or an embedded system platform like **FreeRTOS** or **Zephyr**.
2. **Network Interface**: Use a software or hardware-based network interface (e.g., **NIC driver**).
3. **Simulator**: Use a network simulator like **Wireshark** to observe packet transmission.

### Step 2: Implementing the Ethernet Layer

The Ethernet layer deals with creating frames, managing MAC addresses, and calculating checksums. Once we've implemented the Ethernet frame construction and packet handling, we can move to the next layer.

### Step 3: Implementing the IP Layer

The IP layer manages routing and addressing, taking care of the packets' journey from source to destination. Once the Ethernet frame is built, the IP layer will manage packet forwarding, fragmentation, and header management.

### Step 4: Implementing the Transport Layer (UDP)

The transport layer handles end-to-end communication, providing functionality like multiplexing and de-multiplexing of data. In our example, we'll implement UDP for simplicity, as it allows us to handle basic packet transmission without worrying about the overhead of connection management.

### Step 5: Integrating the Layers

Once the layers are implemented, they need to be integrated. The Ethernet layer will pass packets to the IP layer, which will then forward them to the transport layer. Each layer will handle the packet's specific responsibilities, from addressing to routing to delivering data.

### Step 6: Testing and Debugging

Once the stack is in place, it's time to test. Test with sample packets to check the functionality of each layer. Use network sniffers like Wireshark to capture and inspect the packets. Debug any issues, such as incorrect checksums or address mismatches, by inspecting the packet contents at each layer.

---

## CONCLUSION

In this chapter, we walked through the process of building a custom **network protocol stack** from scratch using assembly language. By breaking down the stack into layers (Ethernet, IP, and UDP), we learned how to implement and test low-level communication protocols. We also explored the importance of planning, coding, testing, and optimizing high-performance applications.

Low-level systems programming remains an essential skill in today's computing landscape, especially for applications that demand speed, efficiency, and direct hardware interaction. By mastering these skills, you will be able to tackle complex systems and build high-performance applications from the ground up.

www.ingramcontent.com/pod-product-compliance
Lightning Source LLC
LaVergne TN
LVHW022347060326
832902LV00022B/4297